SARAH DOUDNEY: SELECTED POEMS AND HYMNS

Teaching and admonishing one another in Psalms, and Hymns, and Spiritual Songs.

Sarah Doudney: Selected Poems and Hymns

Consisting of the poems from
"The Psalms of Life"
and other selections

BY

SARAH DOUDNEY

WITH A PREFACE BY THE
REV. R. H. BAYNES, M.A.,
VICAR OF ST. MICHAEL AND ALL ANGELS, COVENTRY.

COMPLIED BY CHARLES J. DOE

[CURIOSMITH]

MINNEAPOLIS

Published by Curiosmith.
Minneapolis, Minnesota.
Internet: curiosmith.com.

Psalms of Life was previously published by HOULSTON AND SONS, 1871; other poems from *The Sunday Magazine for Family Reading*, 1874–6, 1879–82, 1884–9, and 1892; *Good Words* magazine edited by Rev. Donald Macleod, 1876, 1880, 1882–3, and 1886–7; *Littell's Living Age* magazine, 1875–6, 1880, 1885, and 1890; *Sunday at Home Family Magazine*, 1878–9; *Home Songs for The Quiet Hours* edited by R. H. Baynes, 1878; *Churchman's Shilling Magazine and Family Treasury* conducted by Charles Mackeson, volumes 4, 7, 9, 10, 13, and 16; *A Crown of Flowers*, poems and pictures collected from *The Girls Own Paper* edited by Charles Peters; *Peterson's Magazine*, 1877; various hymnals and other sources. Please note that many of the poems were reprinted from other sources. Sarah Doudney's poetry is scattered far and wide across many periodicals and this collection makes no claim to be comprehensive.

The cover photo is of the Minter Gardens Water Wheel, Chilliwack, B.C. Anonymous attribution from openwalls.com.

Supplementary content, compilation, poetry selection, book layout, and cover design: Copyright © 2017 Charles J. Doe

ISBN 9781946145291

CONTENTS

———o◦⊙◦o———

PSALMS OF LIFE

CONTENTS *(Continued)*

SELECTIONS FROM "THE SUNDAY MAGAZINE"

CONTENTS *(Continued)*

SELECTIONS FROM "GOOD WORDS MAGAZINE"

SELECTIONS FROM "LITTELL'S LIVING AGE"

SELECTIONS FROM HYMNALS

CONTENTS *(Continued)*

MISCELLANEOUS SELECTIONS

Preface to Psalms of Life

I have been asked by my friend, the Author of these "Psalms of Life," to write a preface for her book. I do not think that it needs any preface at all, for it thoroughly explains itself, and will, I believe, find a warm welcome in many a home, and a true response in many a heart. The Hymns are exactly what she has described them, "Psalms of Life." They have been written amid the work and warfare of daily life, and they are full of thoughts and truths which, by God's good blessing, may help us to do earnestly the one, and wage manfully the other. The highest aspiration of the writer will, I know, be attained, if any words of hers shall minister comfort to the sorrowing, hope to the downcast, and strength to the weary. It is in this blessed ministry for good that the real power and value of Hymns seem to me to consist. They form both the poetic Liturgy of the Church, and the precious heritage of each of her separate members. As I once ventured to say elsewhere—in the great congregation of Christ's faithful people, amid the far waste of some colonial land, on shipboard, when the eye and ear can discern nothing save God's stars above, and God's great sea around—in the loneliness of the darkened chamber of sickness, and even up to the margin of the cold river of death, next to the words of Holy Scripture and the deep utterances of the Book of Common Prayer, the Hymns of the Church are most cherished and most dear, lifting up the soul by the very melody of well-remembered words, and soothing it with the sweetness of the blessed truths those words enshrine.

It is no light praise of the "Psalms" that follow, to say that some of them have already been used in the worship of the Church, while others have solaced and cheered some patient sufferers who are not with us now, for their warfare is accomplished, and in the rest of Paradise they behold their Lord.

It only remains to add that most of the "Psalms of Life" have already appeared in periodicals of the day, and that the writer's warm thanks are tendered to those publishers who have so kindly given their permission to reprint her Hymns.[1]

R. H. BAYNES, M.A.

FEAST OF ST. MICHAEL
AND ALL ANGELS, MDCCCLXXI.

---

1 Amongst these, special mention must be made of the Religious Tract Society, Messrs. Cassell and Co., the proprietors of the *Churchman's Shilling Magazine*, and the publishers of "Songs of Gladness."

Christ's Invitation

Incline your ear, and come unto Me: hear, and your soul shall live; and I will make an everlasting covenant with you, even the sure mercies of David.—ISAIAH 55:3.

Come unto Me, and rest,
Thou weary heart, distrest
With wasting toil, and strivings vain and endless;
Mourning from day to day
For idols passed away;—
Come unto Me; I will not leave thee friendless.

I watched thy cisterns fail,
I saw thee spent and pale,
With parched lips, and heart with anguish bursting;
Then, from the desert sod,
Thy cry went up to God;—
Come unto Me; I will not leave thee thirsting.

I watched thee strive to feed
On husks that mocked thy need;
I saw thee faint with weariness and fasting;
No hand thy want supplied,
Thy brethren turned aside;—
Come unto Me; My bread is everlasting.

I watched thy taper gleam
With dim, uncertain beam
Through the long hours of darkness fast declining;
I saw its flame at last
Quenched by the chill night-blast;—
Come unto Me; My light is always shining.

I watched thee stretch thy hands
Across thy barren lands
To harvest-fields where other hands were reaping;
No golden glories crowned
Thy dry and stony ground;—
Come unto Me; I will not leave thee weeping.

Christ's Invitation

For thee I lived and died;
  Behold My Hands,—My Side
Pierced for thy sake;—hast thou not heard the story?
  Mark well My Crown of thorn,
  My Body bruised and torn;—
Come unto Me, and thou shalt share My glory.

"Thinking of Jesus"

A poor woman who was dying said in her last hours, "I can do nothing for myself—I cannot even read the Bible; so I lie here, thinking of Jesus."

The year is near its end, and hoar frost blanches
    Green turf and dark brown slopes at morning prime,
Sorrowful winds go sighing through the branches,
    Where amber leaves yet linger for a time;
Virginian creepers hang their scarlet fringes
    Athwart old crumbling walls, grown worn and grey—
And solemnly their dying glory tinges
    Yon window with the beauty of decay.

Dim eyes look through the narrow cottage casement,
    Where dark red roses on their slender stalks
Bow down their heavy heads in self-abasement,
    And drop their petals on the moss-grown walks;
Dim eyes—whose glances nevermore shall brighten
    At sight of young spring blossoms in their bloom,
Nor need the gleam of primroses to lighten
    The dull grey shadows of the little room.

She will not view those upland fields snow-shrouded,
    Nor mark the fair frost-tracery on the pane,
Nor watch the sky by winter gloom o'erclouded,
    Nor see the Christmas stars shine out again.
She will not listen to the church bells ringing
    From the old tower their Christmas greeting sweet,
Nor hear the clear child-voices blithely singing
    Their ancient carols through the village street.

Yet through the long, long hours, while strength is wasting,
    She lieth calmly in the shadows dim,
"Thinking of Jesus," every moment hasting
    Nearer and nearer unto home and Him;
"Thinking of Jesus," when the moonbeams soften
    The room's harsh outlines with a touch of grace;

"Thinking of Jesus"

"Thinking of Jesus,"—meekly praying often
   That ere the day dawn she may see His face.

Her life hath been a time of toil and weeping,
   Few sunbeams came to make her pathway bright;
Her hands have sown, while other hands were reaping;
   Her heart was sad, while other hearts were light.
Forgotten by the world—by friends forsaken,
   In the hard struggle for her daily bread;
Yet her meek trust in God remained unshaken,
   "Thinking of Jesus," she was comforted.

Ah! there are many in the world's high places
   Whose minds are filled with thoughts of selfish schemes,
Who wear the weary shadow on their faces,
   That comes of blighted hopes and broken dreams;
Could they but stand beneath this roof so lowly,
   And see the work that Christ's dear love can do,
Making the dying spirit calm and holy,
   Would they not long to think of Jesus too?

Thinking of Him, no earthly hand shall sever
   Her soul's firm tendrils from the living Vine;
For faith shall hold Him fast, and trust Him ever—
   Not even death can make that clasp untwine!
Give me such confidence, Thou blest Redeemer,
   Teach me to love Thee with unwearied zest,
That I, no more a vain, bewildered dreamer,
   "Thinking of Jesus," may find peace and rest.

"A Place Called Gethsemane"

"By Thine agony and bloody sweat; by Thy cross and passion; by Thy precious death and burial; by Thy glorious resurrection and ascension; and by the coming of the Holy Ghost, good Lord, deliver us."

Lonely Gethsemane,
   My spirit turns to thee
From this poor world of perishable bloom;
   Seeking thy dusky bowers,
   I muse in silent hours,
'Mid the dim shadow of thine olive gloom.

For me, O Christ, for me,
   That pallid Brow I see
Steeped in thick night-dew,—pressed upon the sod;
   For me, for me, I know
   That Head was bowed so low
In Thy great conflict, O Thou Son of God!

Visions of coming woes
   In that dread hour arose;—
A spectral Cross upon a darkened hill,—
   A maddened, mocking throng,—
   A Victim borne along,—
Thou sawest all, and Thou wert willing still.

Down in that sombre glade
   The paschal moonbeams strayed
Through the deep leafy silence brooding there:
   Silvered the olive boughs,
   And bound those sacred brows
With a pale ring of glory, dim and fair.

Did not Thine eyes foresee
   Another crown—for Thee,
Woven of thorns, and wet with crimson dew?
   O Love, so sorely tried,
   That would not set aside
The pangs which Thine omniscient soul foreknew!

Ah! when this fevered life
    Draws me within its strife,
And holds me in its silken web of lies,
    Lead me awhile with Thee
    To sad Gethsemane,
Where the dark branches quivered to Thy sighs.

    Break Thou the charmèd sleep,
    And give me strength to keep
Watch with my Lord one hour, that I may see
    A little of that woe
    From whence my bliss shall flow,
And know the pain that won such joy for me.

    Yea, Jesus, even more;
    If Thy dear Hand should pour
Into my cup a draught of deadly wine,
    Let me, for Thy sweet sake,
    The bitter chalice take,
Saying, "Thy will be done, O Lord—not mine!"

    So shall this moonlit shade
    Dearer to me be made
Than the marred beauty of old Eden bowers;
    Dearer the midnight breeze
    That stirs those solemn trees
Than the rich breath of June's full-blossomed flowers.

    Lonely Gethsemane,
    My spirit turns to thee,
Seeking thy silent, angel-haunted sod,
    In that far Eastern land
    Where yet His feet shall stand
When men shall know Him for the Son of God.

The Knight's Tomb

It is sown in dishonor; it is raised in glory:
It is sown in weakness; it is raised in power:
It is sown a natural body; it is raised a spiritual body.

Here in the old side-chapel, calmly lying
    With hands crossed meekly as a sign of grace,
And ruby gleams from yon rich window dyeing
    The cold white pallor of his sculptured face;

He sleepeth well; the tender light hath crowned him
    With a dim aureole of golden mist;
And the grey shadows ever shifting round him
    Are touched by changeful tints of amethyst.

Day after day the deep prayer-music pealing
    Through mighty arches, rolls above his breast;
And flute-like notes from boyish voices stealing
    Seem but to lull him into calmer rest.

But who can tell the passion and the anguish,
    The long, sad watch that came before the sleep?
How often did his knightly spirit languish
    In the stern vigil it was doomed to keep!

The sword and shield in deadly fight were dinted
    Ere Death's low tones might bid the conflict cease,
And God's white angel with a touch imprinted
    On that worn brow his seal of perfect peace.

And we the living, who with quiet paces
    Come here to gaze upon his marble bed,
Bringing our restless hearts and care-lined faces
    So near the hallowed slumber of the dead;

We too must know the striving and the failing,
    The daily war with unrelenting foes,
Until, by heavenly might at last prevailing,
    We gain the victory, and earn repose:

The Knight's Tomb

Resting until the trump of resurrection
   Awakes us at the Lord's appointed hour,
And our own bodies clad in full perfection,
   Once sown in weakness, shall be raised in power.

First the long strife—the sleep—and then the waking,
   The sudden change from peace to ecstasy,
When we, the image of our Maker taking,
   Shall wear His likeness through eternity.

"One of the Songs of Sion"

"And again they said, Alleluia."

Down below me lay the fertile acres,
    By the mellow sunshine warmly kissed;
Far away I saw the white sea-breakers
    Glimmer through a veil of gauzy mist.

Down below me lay the wooded valleys,
    Shrining village homes and rural loves
In the quiet of their cool green alleys,
    Haunted by the murmur of the doves.

Sunlit slopes with shady purple tinges,
    Furzy commons stretching free and wide;
Solitary pools with reedy fringes,
    Where the moorhen and the plover hide.

At my feet, like filmy fairy tangles,
    Silken webs athwart the turf were spread;
And, like gems, the wonderful dew spangles
    Flashed and glittered on each slender thread.

Up above me rose the hill-top, crested
    By an ancient church, all grey and worn;
And I paused for weariness, and rested
    In the glory of the early morn.

Sunlight on the summer world was lying,
    Darkness veiled my spirit like a shroud!
And I prayed in bitter sorrow, crying
    For the light that shines behind the cloud.

Then I wept and listened, waiting, pleading,
    Hoping vainly for an answering word;
But the soft south wind swept by unheeding,
    And the harebells quivered, lightly stirred.

Bright-winged butterflies around me fluttered,
    Bees were booming through the golden air,

"One of the Songs of Sion"

While the troubled soul within me uttered
    All her passion in a voiceless prayer.

Lo! a sudden strain of music straying
    Downwards from the church's open door
Hushed the bitter words my heart was saying,
    Chased away the cloud for evermore!

Children's voices through the stillness ringing,
    Drifted softly far across the sod;
Children's voices—gladly, sweetly singing
    Alleluia to the praise of God.

As a sign of tender love and pity
    Came the hallowed tones and lingered long;
Like a message from the Golden City,
    Blending with the notes of earthly song.

Deep into the spirit's darkest regions
    Flashed the light, let in by that sweet hymn:
"Alleluia," sing the white-robed legions,
    "Alleluia," chant the seraphim!

As the sick man, on his weary pillow,
    Listens for the herald of the dawn;
Hears the low breeze rustle through the willow,
    Hears the grasses whisper on the lawn;

Knowing surely that the gentle warning,
    Lightly breathed by winds upon the earth,
Is the mystic harbinger of morning,
    Wafted from the chambers of her birth;

So the soul, in Lenten darkness shrouded,
    Hears the songs of Sion chanted here,
Surest tokens of that dawn unclouded,
    Soon to burst upon our shadowed sphere.

Surest tokens of the music breaking
    In great waves upon the glassy sea,
Where the minstrels of the Lord are waking
    Anthems of eternal melody.

The Communion of Saints

And we also bless Thy holy name for all Thy servants departed this life in Thy faith and fear; beseeching Thee to give us grace so to follow their good examples, that with them we may be partakers of Thy heavenly kingdom.

The night steals on apace, and white mists creep
    Over low-lying fields and valleys still;
The crimson sky grows dull, and shadows deep
    Gather beneath the hill.

Slowly I see the heavens unfold afar,
    Like dusky purple curtains softly drawn
Asunder, and one tremulous bright star
    Steps out to watch till dawn.

The breezes sleep, but autumn flower-scents roam,
    With mystic sweetness in each wandering breath,
As if to tell us of the angels' home,
    Where there is no more death.

And thoughts of that far-distant spirit-land
    Fill us with longings, till we pine to see
The faces of the lost, and understand
    Our life's great mystery.

This we believe, our risen Lord above
    Hath knit together in one holy bond
The Church on earth, whose very name we love,
    With the great Church beyond.

With angels and archangels, and with all
    The company of heaven, do we praise;
But theirs are now the endless festival,
    And ceaseless holy days.

Ours are the Alleluias faint and brief,
    The Sundays that like gems lie far apart;

The Communion of Saints

The "Miserere" chanted low, when grief
    Burdens the feeble heart.

Ours is the love for those beyond the strife,
    We thank Him in the words well known and dear,
For all His saints departed from this life
    In His own faith and fear.

Ours are the shadows and the gloom of Lent,
    And the brief joy while Easter glories shine;
The comfort of Christ's blessed Sacrament,
    His flesh and blood divine.

Theirs is the shade no longer, but the light
    That never fades, and Jesu's presence sweet
Revealed not only unto faith, but sight,
    Perfect, and most complete.

It is but death's dark curtains that divide
    The saints above from those they loved so well;
Friends may still wander with us side by side,
    Near, but invisible;—

May still at times be suffered to return
    To the old haunts they knew in years gone by,
Though human eyes are powerless to discern
    These spirit-watchers nigh.

In the unbroken calm of evening hours,
    Perchance they walk on earth with noiseless tread;
They whisper to us in the sighs of flowers,
    Saying, "Be comforted;

"We too have trod the sad world's thorny way,
    Have borne, as ye do now, the secret grief;
Have seen our earthly hopes, like yours, decay,
    And fade as doth a leaf.

"And we have won the rest that ye shall win;
    Hereafter ye shall sing the song of praise

That all Christ's children, who have come within
   The Church Triumphant, raise."

"Still the Church Militant must watch and wait,
   With eager eyes turned ever to the east;
Until the Bridegroom opes the golden gate,
   And calls her to the feast."

Organic Notes

A song and melody, in our heaviness.

Echoes of cathedral music
    Heard, it may be, long ago,
Linger with us unforgotten,
    Haunt us still, and live and grow;
They are drifting, softly drifting
    Through the wild unrest of life,
Golden organ notes, uplifting
    Weary souls above the strife.

Though the clamour of the city
    Round our outer being rolls,
Still those sacred notes are filling
    All the chambers of our souls;
As if touched by hands immortal,
    Stray chords, tremulous with love,
Drifted through some open portal
    Of the wondrous Church above!

In the grey and silent morning,
    Ere the shadows are withdrawn,
When the white mist hides the valley
    With a veil of airy lawn;
Then we listen, hearing slowly
    Through the stillness deep and calm,
Murmurs of that music holy,
    Like the cadence of a psalm.

When the summer sunset lingers
    Low adown the crimson west,
And the weary hands are folded
    With the blessed sense of rest;
Then we listen, strengthened, soothèd
    By the magic of that strain,
Till the furrowed brow is smoothèd,
    And the heart grows young again.

Organ Notes

They are drifting, softly drifting
    Through the great world's daily strife,
Golden organ notes that tell us
    Of a new and better life;
Low, clear music, sweetly blending
    With the spirit's voiceless cry;
Undertones that have no ending,
    Echoes of eternity!

The Crown of Patience

If thou wilt not suffer, thou refusest to be crowned; but if thou desirest to be crowned, fight manfully, and endure patiently.
—THOMAS A KEMPIS.

I knelt before mine Holy One
 In spring-tide's early days;
I worshipped there, the very air
 Was tremulous with praise!
The song of birds was in the land,
 The wind was cool and sweet;
I carried lilies in mine hand,
 And laid them at His feet.
Then in that morning light He smiled
 As thus He spake to me—
"Lo, as the lily among thorns
 Must My beloved be."

I knelt before mine Holy One
 In summer's balmy hours;
The winds were hushed, the earth was flushed
 With lavish bloom of flowers:
I heard the murmur of the dove
 In forest arches dim;
And as a token of my love
 A rose I brought to Him.
Then in that golden light He smiled
 As thus He spake to me—
"Lo! I alone am Sharon's Rose,
 That blossomed once for thee."

I knelt before mine Holy One
 When songs of joy were borne
From fruitful lands, where busy hands
 Were binding up the corn:
The wild flowers drooped upon the plain
 Beneath the languid heat;

I brought an ear of golden grain,
   And laid it at His feet.
Then in that mellow light He smiled
   As thus He spake to me,—
"I only am the Bread of Life,
   And I will nourish thee."

I knelt before mine Holy One
   When all my hopes were dead;
On field and height, a shroud of white
   The silent snows had spread:
No flower was left to live forlorn
   And brave the bitter blast;
I wove a coronal of thorn,
   And brought my Lord at last.
Then in that dreary light He smiled
   As thus He spake to me—
"This is the crown, the cruel crown,
   That once I wore for thee.

"Go, bind the chaplet round thy brows,
   And wear it for My sake;
With faith and prayer thy slender share
   Of sorrow meekly take!
Mine hand shall aid thee in thy need,
   My love shall hold thee up;
But as thou art Mine own indeed,
   Thy lips shall taste My cup:
Bear on awhile, My tender care
   Shall guard thee day and night,
And give thee for thy crown of thorns
   A diadem of light."

The Children's Angels

Some have entertained angels unawares.

Here lies the village in its nest of green,
  With plumy pine trees ever sighing round;
And through dark boughs you catch the silver sheen,
  And hear the river-sound:

While clamorous crows across the lowlands call,
  Blotting the cloudless sky with sable wings;
Or perching idly on the grey church wall,
  Where fibrous ivy clings.

Here stands the old farmhouse, with moss-grown eaves,
  Where sparrows chirp, and building martins hide;
Its porch a very bower of dancing leaves,
  Its casements opened wide.

Above the golden thatch the sweet-briar flings
  Its long green arms, and pink, shell-tinted flowers;
And soft bird-music from the garden rings
  Through long, long summer hours.

Here in the doorway framed in shifting shade,
  Mary, the meek house-mother, calmly sits;
While round her brows the mellow light hath made
  A glory as she knits.

Swift glide her glancing needles to and fro,
  Her ball of yarn moves softly at her feet;
Her cheeks are pale, her locks are white as snow,
  Her eyes are strangely sweet.

Something outlived and something yet to come
  Have set on her calm face the seal it wears;
You know that when those patient lips are dumb
  Her soul is full of prayers.

The Children's Angels

Ask for the story that she loves to tell,
    The simple tale of comfort born in pain;
A dream perchance it may be called—ah, well,
    Such dreams are not in vain!

"I had three children, sir; five years ago
    A fever came, and swept my two away;
It was to me a time of frenzied woe,
    I could not weep nor pray.

"No tender thought of comfort came to me,
    And I grew hard and thankless in my grief;
The cruel wind had stripped my household tree,
    And left but one small leaf.

"I languished in the stillness of the house,
    I missed the tiny shouts and words and cries;
My one wee darling—quiet as a mouse,
    Watched me with large, sad eyes.

"I missed them in the budding days of spring,
    I missed them when I saw the ripe nuts fall;
But when the Christmas chimes began to ring,
    I missed them most of all!

"On Christmas evening in yon little room
    My child lay sleeping on her father's knee,
My goodman slumbered too; and awful gloom
    Had settled down on me.

"Without—I heard the Christmas carols sung;
    Within—I only saw those vacant chairs;
Ah me! I shivered in my woe, and wrung
    My wild hands unawares!

"And was I dreaming, sir?—I scarcely know
    (The carols sounded louder in the street):
But a bright angel, white as driven snow,
    Sat in each darling's seat.

"I cannot tell, it might have been a dream,
　　But from that hour mine agony was past;
Angels were in the house—I caught the gleam
　　Of wings around me cast.

"One blossom springeth when another dies,
　　The wild rose blushes in the hawthorn's place;
Nought lieth waste—for Nature's hand supplies
　　Each void with fresher grace.

"And in the heart no blanks unfilled remain,
　　Each empty seat shall have its angel guest;
Our saddest losses bring our highest gain;—
　　Through sorrow cometh rest.

"That is my story, sir; and it may be
　　A doting mother's fancy, vague and wild;
Yet in my soul I know God gave to me
　　An angel for each child."

A Farewell Communion

Lord, I have loved the habitation of Thy house, and the place where Thine honour dwelleth.—PSALM 26:8.

One gleam of rosy fire
Has touched the tall church spire;
And the soft dreamy light of early day
Steals through the ancient street,
Where many weary feet
Have trodden patiently their toilsome way.

And, like an olden rhyme,
The silver-sounding chime
Wakens sweet echoes in the thoughtful breast—
Echoes of other days,
Of peace and prayer and praise,
And tender memories of Sunday rest.

The sweet, sad Autumn weaves
Her crown of crimson leaves,
And a low breeze goes softly singing by;
With airy touch it waves
The grass upon the graves,
And creeps within the old church door to die.

Here, in the quiet aisle,
I pause a little while
To gaze on vaulted roof and column fair,
And watch the fitful shade
By rainbow colours made
On time-worn pavement and on marble stair.

Father and Friend divine,
In this fair house of Thine,
Where oft in fervent prayer Thy child hath bent,
Let special grace come down,
The closing rite to crown,
Be with me now in this last Sacrament.

O Saviour, ever blest,
My soul first tasted rest
In this dear church, where Thou didst first impart
Thyself in wine and bread,
And here sustained and fed,
I held Thy very Presence in mine heart.

Lord Jesus, deign to pour
Thy gift of life once more
Into my spirit ere I leave this place;
Let the last banquet be
Sweetest of all to me,
More richly mingled with Thy love and grace.

Help Thou this feeble heart;
Teach me when I depart
Thy power can reach me o'er life's barren lands;
Not in this church alone
Thy blessings wait Thine own;
Thou dwellest not in temples made with hands.

The poorest house of prayer
Is rich if Thou art there;
When Thou didst celebrate the Paschal Feast,
No pomp of stately gloom
Adorned that "upper room,"
Thou wert Thyself both Sacrifice and Priest.

Do Thou my Guardian be,
Lest I lose sight of Thee
In the fair beauty of Thine earthly fane;
Unless Thy Spirit's might
Direct mine heart aright,
And fix my thoughts on Thee, all else is vain.

Though blessed be these walls,
Wherein my soul recalls
The day of her espousal unto Thee,

A Farewell Communion

A thousand times more blest
Is that beloved Guest
Who in the wilderness will come to me.

"Closer Than a Brother"

I have heard of Thee by the hearing of the ear: but now mine eye seeth Thee.—JOB 42:5.

I.

Enthroned upon the purple-vested hills
    Sat the fair Autumn in her regal glow,
And the clear voices of the silver rills
    Made music down below.

The woods were glorious, but far and near
    The scattered leaves their gleams of scarlet shed,
As if the life-blood of the dying year
    Had stained them ruby-red.

And the strange stillness soothed us more and more
    As on we wandered slowly, hand in hand,
Like lovers in the magic days of yore
    Passing through fairy-land.

For twisted roots of wild fantastic shape
    Haunted our path with limbs of rugged brown;
This seemed a satyr, that a goblin ape
    Wearing an ivy crown.

O friend, we knew that happiness like ours
    Was solemn in its purity, and rare;
Treading the borders of immortal bowers,
    Breathing immortal air!

Then softly as an angel clothed in white
    Came Death, and met us with a placid smile;
Laid on our clasping hands his finger light,
    And whispered, "Part awhile."

II.

Low in the heavens stooped the fiery sun,
    Flushing the peaceful landscape far and wide;
When sudden I became aware of One
    Close walking by my side.

"Closer Than a Brother"

He spake of comfort, but I would not weep,
    Wrapping the chilly mantle of despair
More closely round my stricken soul, to keep
    All hope from entrance there.

At length, grown weary of my woe, I turned
    To gaze awhile on my companion's face;
Ah me! I trembled, for mine eyes discerned
    Thereon a blood-red trace.

"Is this," I said, "the sunset's parting stain
    That casts a rosy shadow on Thy brow?"
But faster fell the drops like crimson rain,
    "Ah, Lord, I know Thee now!

"Forgive the feeble soul that understands
    So little of this wondrous love of Thine."
He answered, holding out His pierced hands,
    "Was any grief like Mine?"

I knelt and kissed my Saviour's wounded feet,
    Like Magdalene I washed them with my tears;
Fast flowed the healing waters fresh and sweet
    From fountains sealed for years.

Then on my trembling lips I felt His kiss,
    I heard His promise of eternal rest;
The world grew darker, but the light of bliss
    Remained within my breast.

The Spirit of God

The wind bloweth where it listeth, and thou hearest the sound thereof,
but canst not tell whence it cometh, and whither it goeth.—JOHN 3:8.
Thou knowest not what is the way of the Spirit.—ECCLESIASTES 11:5.

O soft wind-voices through the pine boughs straying,
    Swinging the plumy branches to and fro;
Who shall declare the words that ye are saying,
    Or follow where ye go?

Ye murmur—and the full-blown blossoms quiver,
    While seeds of life are wafted through the air;
Ye mutter—and the foam-pearls strew the river,
    And tall reeds tremble there.

Great is the Hand that scatters blessings seed-like,
    Whose germs are carried by His Spirit's wings;
Blest is the pliant soul that bendeth reed-like
    Before its whisperings.

O give us grace to hear its mystic sighing,
    To catch the music of its lightest tone;
And let the echo in our hearts replying,
    Thy Spirit-message own.

Grant us Thy power, O Lord, to shape and fashion
    The deed that springs from the imparted thought;
Oh, give us words to speak our poet-passion,
    And tell what Thou hast wrought!

Oh, bend the stubborn knees in meek devotion,
    Oh, bow the haughty souls in humble prayer;
And let Thy rushing wind of pure emotion
    Clear all the tainted air.

Not unto us, O Christ, shall praise be given,
    To Thee be glory for Thy gift divine,
With sin and wrath Thy Spirit's might hath striven,
    And all the work is Thine.

The Spirit of God

The one pure feeling through our darkness drifting,
    White-winged and beautiful as some stray dove,
The sudden prayer our heavy hearts uplifting
      With all the strength of love;

The kind word uttered to the feeble-hearted,
    The bold word spoken that Thy light may shine,
These are the promptings by Thy breath imparted,
      And all the praise is Thine.

O soft wind-voices through the pine-boughs straying,
    We cannot trace the airy paths ye go;
O breath of God, our human spirits swaying,
      Thy way we cannot know!

A Pilgrim's Prayer

"Those things which for our unworthiness we dare not, and for our blindness we cannot ask, vouchsafe to give us for the worthiness of Thy Son, Jesus Christ our Lord. Amen."

Weary and sad tonight,
I look to Thee for light;
Thick darkness rests upon the road I tread;
Let but one beam of Thine
Over the pathway shine,
And Thy poor pilgrim shall be comforted.

Longing for strength and grace,
I strive to see Thy face,
Like some lone worshipper in dim-lit aisle
Seeking with earnest gaze
To pierce the twilight haze
That veils from him the Saviour's pictured smile.

Still for Thy voice I pine,
Catching a word of Thine
As one who hears amid the city's roar
Some low-toned silver note
Of chanting voices float
Forth from the grey cathedral's open door.

Saviour and Brother dear,
I know that Thou art near,
In Thy blest presence would my soul rejoice;
But this dim mortal sight
Can scarce perceive Thy light,
And these dull ears but faintly hear Thy voice.

Watch me and guard me well,
Lest the world's evil spell
Breathed on my faith should make the flame expire;
Strengthen the feeble hands

A Pilgrim's Prayer

To work at Thy commands,
And fill the heart with heavenly desire.

Let me be purified
As gold by fire is tried,
Make me a jewel meet for Thee to wear;
Cleanse Thou my garment's stain,
Let it be white again
As angels' raiment, beautiful and fair.

Sustain me when I sink,
And suffer me to drink
Of living water that I thirst no more;
Over this desert sand
Guide me like Israel's band,
And let Thy cloudy pillar go before.

Give me the power to pray,
Call back the thoughts that stray
On airy wings, in vain unmeaning flight;
Jesus, be all-in-all,
Hold every sense in thrall,
And thrill the soul with infinite delight.

Let faith be granted me
Thy heavenly Face to see,
Mine unbelief alone creates the cloud;
Only my doubts and fears
Keep from my longing ears
The blessed Voice that speaketh clear and loud.

Give me sweet hours of rest,
Leaning upon Thy breast
Like the belov'd disciple; let me be
A favoured child of grace,
Held in my Lord's embrace
Close to the Heart so deeply pierced for me.

Evensong

I will lay me down in peace, and take my rest: for it is Thou, Lord, only, that makest me dwell in safety.—PSALM 4:8.

Sinks the kingly sun in crimson splendour,
　　While the sweet bells chime for evensong;
Comes the evening breeze with murmurs tender
　　Rustling in the churchyard grasses long.

Fall the autumn leaves, with glory painted,
　　Like the tints from chancel windows shed,
Where the vestments of the figures sainted,
　　Blaze with amber glow and ruby red.

Showers of gold and scarlet hide the mosses
　　That have clustered on the churchyard way;
Sunset colours rest upon the crosses,
　　And the hallowed walls so grave and grey.

Drifting through the church's open portal,
　　See the dead leaves scattered on the aisle;
But the Tree of Life hath leaves immortal,
　　We shall pluck them in a little while.

Yonder where the trailing ivy fetters
　　Stones all lichen-grown, and grey with years,
We may trace some broken, worn-out letters,
　　Seen but dimly through our falling tears.

Time will wear away these feeble traces;
　　Names of those released from earthly strife
May be gone from graveyard resting-places,
　　But are written in the Book of Life.

Nothing shall be lost; His promise liveth
　　Through the ages; Jesus Christ will keep
All the Father gave Him, and He giveth
　　His beloved ones the gift of sleep.

But the bells have ceased; the organ pealing
    Calls us with its music deep and strong;
Let us enter here, and meekly kneeling,
    Ask Him to accept our evensong.

Father, let our evening praise ascending
    Unto Thee find favour in Thine eyes:
Jesus! may Thy Holy Spirit blending
    With our prayers, make pure the sacrifice.

Let these weary hearts grow lighter, thinking
    Of the land where there is no more night;
Show the feeble faith, so nearly sinking,
    One bright vision of intense delight!

Let one golden harp-note reach us clearly
    From that white-robed multitude of Thine;
Lift our souls by one faint echo merely
    Of the anthems raised by choirs divine.

Let the angels—who unseen behold us,
    Watching at Thy bidding evermore—
Roll away the shadows that enfold us,
    And reveal one glimpse of yonder shore.

Guard us waking, Saviour, guard us sleeping;
    Let no evil dreams our rest destroy;
Bring us safely through the night of weeping
    To the glory of Thy morn of joy.

Light Above the City

There is sprung up a light for the righteous, and joyful gladness for such as are true-hearted.

Above—soft clouds like tinted snow drifts flying
    Over the quiet sky, so calmly bright;
Beneath—the city with its house-roofs lying
    Veiled by the tender haze of dying light:
Above—the solemn peace, the tranquil glory
    That follows oft a day all dim with showers;
Beneath—the great unrest, the old, sad story,
    The throbbing pulses of this world of ours.

The golden rays grew paler as they drifted
    Down into crowded places foul and dun;
Only the tall spires, out of shadow lifted,
    Caught the last brightness of the sinking sun:
Night hovers in the streets, while daylight lingers
    Still in those upper realms so purely clear—
Weaving her sable shroud with hasty fingers
    To cover every touch of radiance here.

Rich city, with thy gathered heaps of treasure,
    Thy sculptured palaces of regal state,
Where Dives, clad in purple, feasts at pleasure,
    While Lazarus starves unheeded at the gate;
Hast thou no earnest glances, upward tending,
    Which turn from earth to seek this placid sky?
Hast thou no silent breath of prayer ascending
    From human hearts grown sick with vanity?

Yea, from the narrow court and gloomy alley
    Rises the spirit's incense fresh and sweet—
Pure as the sighs of lilies of the valley,
    Whose fragrance floats along the sordid street;
There are wise virgins here, whose lamps are burning
    Through the long vigil with unfailing light;

These watch in patience for the Lord's returning,
   And for His sake they keep their garments white.

They hear a sound of golden harp-notes stealing
   Through the loud tumult of the city's din;
And each repining thought and bitter feeling
   Is silenced by that holy strain within;
With every cry of weariness and sorrow
   Comes the soft music of some undertone,
To tell them of the glorious tomorrow,
   When Jesus Christ shall comfort all His own.

For such as these, the Light above the city
   Is shining even in their darkest hours,
While the gay world, too wild to pause and pity,
   Goes trampling underfoot life's withered flowers,
And the low wail of pain is sadly sighing
   Through the exultant sounds of festal song;
God's faithful children, on His word relying,
   Look upward to His heaven, and grow strong.

These feeble hands the Father deigns to strengthen,
   These wounded hearts He heals with balm of love;
Life's eventide draws on—the shadows lengthen,
   But light still dwells in those pure skies above!
Soon shall the rush of countless angel-pinions
   Sweep through the air; and loud the herald's cry
Shall ring throughout the world's defiled dominions,
   "Behold, O earth, the Bridegroom draweth nigh!"

The Deserted House

We have a building of God, an house not made with hands, eternal in the heavens.—2 CORINTHIANS 5:1.

The old house is deserted;
    And throughout the bleak March day
Come the fitful, sad sea breezes,
    Round its silent walls to play;
And the wild March rains are beating
    On the green lawn, smooth and fair,
While the lonely weeping willow
    Trails its wind-tossed branches there.

No faces at the windows,
    And no footsteps in the hall:
For there broods a sullen silence
    While the shadows rise and fall;
And the restless winds of ocean
    Blowing far across the foam,
Moan a passing wail of pity
    For the place once called a home.

But there were children's voices
    In that house a while ago;
And the sound of little footsteps
    Pattered lightly to and fro;
There where rosy, childish faces
    At the windows often pressed;
And in those dismantled chambers
    Happy children went to rest.

And looking from the casements,
    Youthful dreamers loved to gaze
Far athwart the waste of waters,
    Dim with golden sunset haze;
When the soul was yet unburdened,
    And the fancy wandered free,

The Deserted House

And life's secrets lay unfathomed
    Like the wonders of the sea!

In those dim rooms, together
    Gathered parents, young and old,
When the Christmas psalms were chanted,
    And the Christmas stories told;
When the glow of winter firelight
    Gleams of changeful glory shed
On the grey hairs of the grandsire,
    And the baby's golden head:

And there were secret struggles,
    Mighty battles fought unknown;
For the silent mystic conflict
    Could be seen by God alone;
When the quiet walls have echoed
    To a wounded spirit's cry,
And a mute white face was lifted
    In a prayer of agony.

And there were deep rejoicings
    When the gloomy shades were past,
And the glimmer of the day-dawn
    Broke upon the soul at last;
O the strange unwritten stories
    That these silent chambers hold!
O the mysteries of passion
    That no language shall unfold!

Time worketh wondrous changes,
    And the lone heart weepeth sore
O'er the goodly halls, deserted
    By the guests that come no more;
And it sees not at its threshold
    How the Saviour, knocking, stands,
How He waits to lead it upward
    To "a house not made with hands."

For He hath many mansions
    In His Father's kingdom bright;
And they need not star nor sunshine,
    For His glory giveth light:
There the peace is never broken,
    For the rest is calm and sweet;
And the scattered gems are gathered,
    And the parted friends shall meet.

Thou knowest, loving Jesus,
    How to our poor homes we cling,
Though the tenants are departed,
    And have left us sorrowing:
Take us quickly to Thy household,
    Hear our spirits' earnest prayer,
That the circle of our dear ones
    May be found unbroken there!

Last Words

Let us labour therefore to enter into that rest.—HEBREWS 4:11.

"Jesus, I wait." Last words breathed soft and low
　　From dying lips grown tremulous and faint:
O Great Life-giver, Thou didst surely know
　　The yearnings of Thy saint.

Waiting—a moment only—just a pause,
　　A hush before the music had begun;
A silence ere the cloudy veil withdraws,
　　And the bright home is won.

"Jesus, I wait." Was He not waiting too,
　　With hands outstretched in welcome, and with eyes
Brimful of love, to guide His servant through
　　The gates of Paradise?

O calm, safe rest! all sorrows passed away
　　Like twilight mists before a risen moon;
O blessed close to life's most weary day!
　　O peace attained so soon!

Teach us to live, and living, wait for Thee,
　　Redeemer—making life and labour sweet;
Watching and working till our eyes shall see
　　The Face they long to greet.

Our highest earthly bliss, to do Thy will;
　　Our hope, the promise of Thy great reward;
Our effort, all Thy purpose to fulfil,
　　And magnify the Lord.

Teach us to wait—as waits the ripened corn
　　In golden fullness for the reaper's hand;
Meet for Thy garner, when the harvest morn
　　Dawns o'er the weary land.

Last Words

And Thou wilt come with radiant angel train,
    Lord of the harvest; claiming all Thine own;
Then shall we greet our dearest ones again,
    And know as we are known.

Then shall the endless festival begin,
    And the long waiting, as a dream, go past;
For love, triumphant over death and sin,
    Shall reign supreme at last.

"God Shall Wipe Away All Tears"

"And sorrow and mourning shall flee away."

There are some whose tears are ready;
    There be some who cannot weep,
But with faces calm and steady,
    All their keenest sorrows keep:
Those, like April clouds, soon breaking
    Into brief and sudden rain;
These, like frozen rivers fettered
    By the winter's binding chain.

And the tears set soon a-flowing
    May as easily be dried;
But some hearts would break in knowing
    All the woe of tears denied,
Did not He whose tender pity
    Our unspoken anguish hears,
Touch the rock and bring the waters,
    For He knows our need of tears.

Yes, He knoweth; and the blessing
    That our souls have often kept,
When life's cross was sorely pressing,
    Is the brief text, "Jesus wept":
For we hear not that the angels
    Shed one tear for mortal woe,
But our Maker took our nature
    And our sorrows here below.

When the city lay before Him
    With its sun-touched towers so fair,
When the people's shouts rose o'er Him,
    And "hosannas" rent the air;
Saw He not those bright domes glimmer
    Through the mist of tears all dim?
Wept He not in His compassion,
    That they would not come to Him?

"God Shall Wipe Away All Tears"

There be tears too often wasted
    In the early days of youth,
For the wine that palls when tasted,
    For the love that has no truth:
For the dreams that passion nurtures
    In the restless brain and heart,
Till the stern, cold voice of reason
    Bids the dreams and dreamer part.

There be tears for human blindness,
    For the errors of our life,
That have made our love unkindness,
    And have turned our peace to strife;
When we weep o'er self-formed fetters
    That our hands can ne'er undo,
Chafing madly at the bondage
    Which may not be broken through.

There be tears, more sad than any,
    For the good that might have been;
For the squandered moments many,
    For the grain we did not glean
When we lingered in the corn-fields,
    Singing songs till set of sun,
Till the last, last sheaf was gathered,
    And the harvest-time was done.

We are longing, ever yearning
    For the time when Thou wilt reign,
A triumphant King returning
    To Thy waiting bride again;
When Thou comest in Thy glory
    To begin the world's new day,
And the tears from off all faces
    Thy dear Hand shall wipe away.

Spring Thoughts

*O all ye green things upon the earth, bless ye the Lord: praise Him
and magnify Him for ever.*

I saw the light of spring lie broad and soft
    On rich brown furrows tinged with emerald hue,
And pure white clouds were drifting far aloft
    O'er a wide sea of blue.

Between the ferny banks all green and moist,
    I wandered slowly down a sheltered way,
Hearing the mavis piping dulcet-voiced
    His ancient roundelay.

The strength of spring is in the swelling buds,
    And a dim greenness clothes the naked trees;
Amid the mosses gleam like ivory studs
    The wood-anemones.

A golden touch unbinds the captive rill,
    The angry winds have ceased their bitter strife;
This world that lay so mute, and cold, and still,
    Has passed from death to life.

We had long patience, Father, for Thy spring,
    We sat in tears, or lifted up our hands
With passionate prayers to hear Thy minstrels sing
    Throughout our silent lands.

And it hath come, the sweet hope long deferred;
    The truth of Thine old promise seems revealed
In rapturous warblings of each happy bird,
    In green blades of the field.

Could we not trust Thee when our woods were bare,
    And Thy cloud-curtains hid the genial light?
While snowflakes whirling through the wintry air
    Buried our dead from sight?

Spring Thoughts

Only at times our fretful hearts have traced
   Thy purpose in the storm-cloud and the rain,
Knowing the Hand that laid our fair earth waste
     Could make it bloom again.

And yet, beneath the snow-shroud white and chill
   The hidden germs of life lay safe and deep;
And all Thy vital laws were working still,
     Though we might doubt and weep.

Has not our feeble faith Thy Spirit grieved?
   Have we not wearied Thee with thankless sigh,
Forgetting all Thy blessed gifts received
     In fruitful days gone by?

O give us grace in surest hope to dwell,
   Until Thy love shall clothe each barren spot!
Teach us to feel Thou doest all things well,
     Although we see Thee not.

Trial

If in the palmy hours of youth,
    Thy life's fair morning-tide,
Thou tremblest at the mimic waves
    O'er which thy bark must glide,
What wilt thou do when Jordan's flood
    Swells in its angry might,
And the clear azure of the skies
    Is changed to darkest night?

If in the sunny land of peace
    Wherein thou trustest now,
Thy heart is vexed when blossoms fall
    From some o'erladen bough,
What wilt thou do when all thy flowers
    Lie desolate and dead,
And the sere leaves of withered hopes
    Rustle beneath thy tread?

If at some passing April shower
    Through which the sunlight shines,
Thy chafing spirit murmurs sore,
    Thy wayward will repines,
What wilt thou do when winter rain
    Beats wildly on thy breast,
Without a single shelter near
    To give thee peace and rest?

If in these tranquil days of ours
    Thy weak hand fears to raise
The holy symbol of thy faith,
    Or speak thy Master's praise,
What wilt thou do in coming years,
    If some with sword and flame

Trial

Should dare thee boldly to confess
    The Saviour's worthy Name?

O thank the Father if His love
    Hath led thy pilgrim feet
Along a safely sheltered way,
    Through pastures green and sweet;
A sterner, darker path *they* knew,
    Those saints of high renown;
For he must bear the martyr's pain
    Who wins the martyr's crown!

Beyond dark Jordan's rolling waves
    The Golden City lies,
And from its pearly portals wide
    Float holy melodies;
The voices of the ransomed there
    Ring o'er death's swelling tide;
Lift up thy head; be strong—thou too
    Shalt reach the other side!

Listen! they sing the Lamb's new song!
    In bitter, bygone years
They learned the prelude of that strain
    With sighs and woe and tears;
They learned it here with breaking hearts
    In scorn and sorrow then;
But angels swell the chorus now,
    And join the grand Amen.

Roll on, dark Jordan; not the force
    Of gathered wave on wave
Can keep one feeble pilgrim back
    Whom Jesus died to save;
Roll on—the silver voices soar
    Above thy troubled foam,
That those who breast thy tide may hear
    The music of their home.

"Truly My Hope Is Even in Thee"

"The more the outward man decayeth, strengthen him, we beseech Thee, the more continually with Thy grace and Holy Spirit in the inner man."

Yes, I am waiting, very calmly waiting
    Until the silver cord is loosed; I know,
By weariness increased and strength abating,
    That Death comes quickly: it is better so.

Familiar things are round me, all unchanging
    With the great change that stealeth over me;
From bough to bough the birds I loved are ranging,
    The violets bloom beneath my favourite tree.

How strange it seems thou wilt flow on, bright river,
    Winding thy silver course through valleys fair;
While on thy breast the golden sunbeams quiver,
    And the white lilies float serenely there.

Still the west wind will murmur to the larches
    With the old music I have known so long,
That stirred the tracery of sylvan arches,
    And filled the pauses in the blackbird's song.

I know the carpet of the shady dingle
    Is thick with moss, and many a primrose gem;
There hyacinths and wavy fern-plumes mingle,
    And village children go to gather them.

They bring them to the Church, where willing fingers
    The buds and blossoms busily entwine;
And gladly o'er the work each spirit lingers—
    But Easter wreaths will own no touch of mine.

Oft I have pictured in my silent dreaming
    That ancient house of prayer on Easter morn,
With the rich light through jewelled windows streaming
    On the frail symbols of the woodlands born!

While every Christian soul therein rejoices
    To sing Thy praise, O Lord of power and might!
And the great volume of the chanting voices
    Mingles with those that "rest not day nor night."

Yea, theirs will be the Feast—the Body broken,
    The precious Wine that hath so oft sufficed
To cheer sad hearts; the benediction spoken,
    The mystic presence of the risen Christ.

Do Thou, O living Lord, my darkness lighten,
    Make Thou a temple of my lonely room;
And let one sunbeam of Thy glory brighten
    These long, long hours of weariness and gloom.

I will be patient till the summons reach me,
    That calls me evermore with Thee to dwell;
But ere I go, I pray Thee, Father, teach me
    To value here Thy gift unspeakable.

Lead me a little while beside still waters,
    And let my soul in Thy green pastures feed;
Till with Thy ransomed flock, Thy sons and daughters,
    I go where Thou fulfillest all my need.

Then though this mortal flesh, because of weakness,
    Permits me not in yon dear Church to be,
I yet may hope, with reverence and in meekness,
    That Thou, my great High Priest, wilt come to me!

"Deliver Us from Evil"

Hold Thou me up, and I shall be safe.—PSALM 119:117.

Lord of Thy church, we pray
That Thou wilt guard our feet from evil snares;
Let no temptations overtake today
Thy children unawares.

Keep us from hurtful things,
And fill our souls so full of love and grace,
That worldly thoughts, and vain imaginings
May find no vacant place.

Deliver us from pride;
Teach us, Thou lowly One, to learn of Thee,
That we in meekness ever may abide,
And deep humility.

Keep us from unbelief;
Let not the feeble flame of faith expire;
Breathe on the soul so dim with doubt and grief,
And kindle holy fire.

Deliver us from strife;
Let not our words like poisoned arrows fly,
But bid us look upon Thy blameless life,
Thy perfect charity.

Keep us from craven fear,
That makes us shrink to wear Thy holy sign;
Rather let grateful hearts that hold Thee dear
Exult in being Thine.

Thus let us follow Thee
Humbly and prayerfully, through joy or shame;
And teach us so to live, that we may be
Worthy of Thy dear Name.

In Time of Sickness

I will be glad, and rejoice in Thy mercy: for Thou hast considered my trouble, and hast known my soul in adversity.—PSALM 31:7.

Saviour, in mine hours of pain
    Send Thy Comforter to me;
All my sorrow shall be gain,
    If it brings one smile from Thee;
In the time of sharp distress
Let me prove Thy tenderness.

When this weary brow is worn
    By an anguish sore and keen,
Jesus, show Thy crown of thorn,
    Teach me what Thy woe hath been;
O Thou Sufferer divine,
Was there any grief like Thine?

Set Thy precious Cross on high,
    Show Thy sacred Wounds afresh;
Thine was human agony,
    Thou didst suffer in the flesh:
Saviour, when Thy pangs are shown,
Shall I not forget mine own?

Let this restless soul grow calm
    When Thy proofs of love I see;
Pour Thy crimson Blood as balm
    On the heart that longs for Thee:
Lamb of God, if Thou art near,
Even sorrow will be dear.

In Thy holy Church today
    Let Thy blessed Spirit wait;
Father, hear when Christians pray
    For the sick and desolate;
Comfort those who cannot share
In Thy sacred service there.

In Time of Sickness

Thou canst raise an altar up,
  Even in this heart of mine;
There Thy grace can fill the Cup
  With Thy life-restoring Wine;
And my hungry soul is fed
By Thine everlasting Bread.

Then these hours of pain shall be
  Hours of holiness and love;
Hours of fellowship with Thee,
  Visions of Thy bliss above;
Wings, wherewith my soul may rise
To the joys of paradise.

Christmas Chimes

Thanks be unto God for His unspeakable Gift.
—2 Corinthians 9:15.

The winds are hushed, and pallid sunbeams glisten
    On the dark ivy and the crystal snow;
Chime on, sweet bells, while Christian spirits listen
    To strains of long ago.

And who can say what tender recollections
    Of happy hours, and sorrowful farewells,
Voices long hushed, and slumbering affections,
    Are wakened by the bells?

Our powers decay, our voices fail and alter,
    Time mars the music of the sweetest tongue;
Theirs are the tones that never change nor falter,
    Old, and yet always young.

They bear today the ancient consolation;
    A message "of great joy" their chime imparts,
Stirring, with mystical reverberation,
    Thousands of weary hearts.

Listen—they speak to thee, O mourning mother!
    The Father will not leave thee all alone;
One hope is taken, but He gives another,
    The Christ-child is thine own.

A new-born babe, He cometh, meek and lowly,
    To fill the void within thine aching breast;
To soothe thee with His love, so deep and holy,
    And give thee perfect rest.

They speak to thee, O dreamer brokenhearted,
    Whose earthly lights have paled, or ceased to shine;
Why dost thou weep for fickle beams departed,
    When Jacob's Star is thine?

Christmas Chimes

Lift up thine eyes; that Light of Life immortal
   Shall chase all shadows from thy rugged way,
Guiding thy feet to heaven's golden portal,
     Turning thy night to day.

Chime on, sweet bells, your Christmas greetings flinging
   Like precious pearls upon the weary earth;
The world is sad; but faith and hope up-springing,
     Shall hail Messiah's birth.

St. Michael and All Angels

"Mercifully grant that as Thy holy Angels always do Thee service in heaven, so by Thy appointment they may succour and defend us on earth."

A warm September sunset richly shading
    The furrowed uplands with a golden gleam;
And far away the dim hill-purples fading
    Into a dusky dream.

An autumn peace on all the landscape sleeping,
    Sweeter than summer light or bloom of spring;
And this low wind, across the meadow sweeping,
    Sounds like an angel's wing.

Ay, surely they are near us—angel legions
    Are drifting downwards through the quiet air,
Bearing glad tidings from immortal regions
    To earth-born sons of care.

O everlasting God, Who hast ordainèd
    These bright-winged ministers to do Thy will,
Let them be with us when our faith hath wanèd,
    To watch and comfort still.

Thou knowest all our conflict—all the failing
    Of flesh and spirit lured by evil powers,
The sore temptations these poor hearts assailing
    In our unguarded hours.

The bitter strife—the conquest won so dearly,
    The feeble strength that seems so fiercely tried;
Thou knowest all—O Father, show us clearly
    The bright ones on our side!

Show us the serried ranks that ever cluster
    Round the baptizèd children of the Lord;
Each with white robes that never lose their lustre,
    And adamantine sword!

St. Michael and All Angels

So shall we fear no evil: living, dying,
    Our souls are in Thy care, Thou wilt defend
The faithful servants on Thy love relying,
    Even until the end.

The Christian's "Good Night"

The early Christians were accustomed to bid their dying friends "Good night!" so sure were they of their awaking at the Resurrection morning.

Sleep on, beloved, sleep and take thy rest,
Lay down thy head upon thy Saviour's breast;
We love thee well, but Jesus loves thee best;—
        Good night!

Calm is thy slumber as an infant's sleep;
But thou shalt wake no more to toil and weep;
Thine is a perfect rest, secure and deep;—
        Good night!

Until the shadow from this earth is cast,
Until He gathers in His sheaves at last,
Until the Lenten gloom is overpast;—
        Good night!

Until the Easter glory lights the skies,
Until the dead in Jesus shall arise,
And He shall come—but not in lowly guise;—
        Good night!

Until, made beautiful by love divine,
Thou in the likeness of thy Lord shalt shine,
And He shall bring that golden crown of thine;—
        Good night!

Only "Good night!" beloved, not "Farewell!"
A little while, and all His saints shall dwell
In hallowed union, indivisible;—
        Good night!

Until we meet again before His throne,
Clothed in the spotless robe He gives His own;
Until we know, even as we are known;—
        Good night!

Take Up Thy Cross

In the world ye shall have tribulation.—JOHN 16:33.

"Take up thy cross, and follow Me,"
    (Dost thou not hear thy Saviour say?)
"And as thy day thy strength shall be,
    I am the Life, the Truth, the Way.
An easy path, a flowery road,
    Behold, I have not promised thee;
But I will help thee bear thy load:
    Take up thy cross, and follow Me.

"Storm-tossed, or scorched by noontide heat,
    Press on across the desert lone;
With aching brow and bleeding feet,
    I lead thee on by ways unknown:
A life of woe and strife and fears
    Thy course on earth must ever be,
But I will wipe away thy tears:
    Take up thy cross, and follow Me.

"I give thee neither gold nor gem,
    No earthly treasure thou shalt share;
Mine is a thorny diadem,
    And such must all My servants wear;
But far above the starry height,
    Within the home prepared for thee,
Thy crown of glory glitters bright:
    Take up thy cross, and follow Me.

"My little flock, a weary band
    By foes and trials sore distressed,
Must journey to the promised land,
    And trust My love to give them rest:
Streams from the smitten rock shall flow,
    And angels' food thy bread shall be;
For all thy need I surely know:
    Take up thy cross, and follow Me."

Yea, Lord, we come our cross to take;
  O give us grace to watch and pray!
Content to suffer for Thy sake,
  Content to tread Thy rugged way;
O strengthen every trembling heart
  That longs yet fears Thine own to be;
Speak Thou, and bid our doubts depart:
  We will leave all, and follow Thee.

A Morn of Joy

The oil of joy for mourning, the garment of praise for the spirit of heaviness.—ISAIAH 61:3.

Here in the old church porch we meet again
    After long years; it seems like some sweet story,
For us, whose paths so long apart have lain,
    To stand together in June's early glory!
Fair looks the land about us: o'er the scene
    Float some light mists, the summer's airy gauzes;
And strangely solemn, coming in between
    Our talk, the old church bells fill up the pauses.

I have come hither very sore of heart
    On many bygone Sundays, praying only
For strength to bear my cross and do my part
    In life, although my way were dark and lonely;
And God hath sent His Comforter, until
    The weary mind of half its load was lightened;
And I walked homewards through the woodland still,
    With stronger hope; and faith restored and brightened.

Now the old grief is ended: but I take
    My present happiness in grateful quiet;
Yet in past years I know such bliss would make
    Each pulse within me beat in rapturous riot;
But those wild days are gone, and better far
    Is this deep sober gladness—calmer, purer
Than the outpourings of youth's first hopes are;—
    Those joys may be more ardent—these are surer.

Let us thank God together; we shall feel
    More fitted for this happier existence,
If at its opening, side by side we kneel,
    And see past troubles in the fading distance;
And He who gave us His unfailing care
    Through wasting years, and held us in His keeping,

A Morn of Joy

Will teach us in humility to bear
    The morn of joy, as the long night of weeping.

Listen—the organ's swelling waves of sound
    Summon the worshippers to prayer and praises;
The place whereon we stand is holy ground,
    For here the dead sleep on beneath the daisies,
While we, the living, bless Thee, gracious Lord,
    With feeble lips and utterance faint and broken;
Thou wilt despise us not, we oft have poured
    Into Thine ear heart-breathings never spoken!

This day shall never be forgotten; when
    The mortal shall have put on the immortal,
And the freed spirit, all untrammelled then,
    Escapes the limits of life's narrow portal;
As now we enter His own church today,
    We ask, while faith and love our souls embolden,
To pass as calmly from Time's shadows gray
    Into thy gates, Jerusalem the Golden!

The Lesson of the Water-Mill

But this I say, brethren, the time is short.—1 CORINTHIANS 7:29.

Listen to the water-mill
　　Through the livelong day
How the clicking of its wheel
　　Wears the hours away!
Languidly the autumn wind
　　Stirs the forest leaves,
From the field the reapers sing
　　Binding up their sheaves;
And a proverb haunts my mind
　　As a spell is cast;
"The mill cannot grind
　　With the water that is past."

Autumn winds revive no more
　　Leaves that once are shed,
And the sickle cannot reap
　　Corn once gatherèd;
Flows the ruffled streamlet on,
　　Tranquil, deep, and still;
Never gliding back again
　　To the water-mill:
Truly speaks that proverb old,
　　With a meaning vast—
"The mill cannot grind
　　With the water that is past."

Take the lesson to thyself,
　　True and loving heart;
Golden youth is fleeting by,
　　Summer hours depart;
Learn to make the most of life,
　　Lose no happy day,
Time will never bring thee back
　　Chances swept away!

Leave no tender word unsaid,
    Love while love shall last;
"The mill cannot grind
    With the water that is past."

Work while yet the daylight shines,
    Man of strength and will!
Never does the streamlet glide
    Useless by the mill;
Wait not till tomorrow's sun
    Beams upon thy way,
All that thou canst call thine own
    Lies in thy "today";
Power, and intellect, and health
    May not always last;
"The mill cannot grind
    With the water that is past."

O the wasted hours of life
    That have drifted by!
O the good *that might have been—*
    Lost, without a sigh!
Love that we might once have saved
    By a single word,
Thoughts conceived, but never penned,
    Perishing unheard;—
Take the proverb to thine heart,
    Take, and hold it fast—
"The mill cannot grind
    With the water that is past."

The Hills

Come, for the mists are rising from the vale
    Like clouds of incense from a shrine of prayer;
Come up among the hills, the free strong gale
    Is blowing freshly there.

There blooms the purple heather in its prime,
    There hums the wild bee in its happy flight;
There sound the sheep-bells like a fairy chime,
    Drifting from height to height.

There float the light cloud shadows, and the blue
    Of the eternal dome above is nigh;
There are no leafy boughs to screen from view
    That arch of sapphire sky.

Come, for the wild free solitude is sweet,
    And far below shall lie the world of care;
No sound of strife, no tramp of restless feet
    Can ever reach thee there.

Come when thy soul within thee is opprest
    With vague misgivings and with musings sad,
For in the sense of freedom there is rest—
    The hills shall make thee glad.

Come, for each breath inspires some lofty thought
    When the pure mountain air thy spirit fills;
The lessons that the ancient sages taught
    Were learned among the hills.

Via Dolorosa

Enclosed by ruined walls, a narrow street,
    Spanned here and there by arches grey and worn,
    Haunted by shadows, squalid and forlorn—
Was this the path that bare His blessed feet?

O Son of God, whose human strength gave way
    Beneath the cross upon this cruel road,
    Thy sacred heart sustained a Heavier load,
And bore it bravely through that bitter day!

Our sins once made that path so rough for Thee,
    The weight of our transgressions pressed Thee down;
    Our guilty fingers wove Thy thorny crown,
And nailed Thee, faint and bleeding, to the Tree.

Ah, Lord! we too our rugged path must tread
    In Lenten bitterness and anguish sore,
    But Thou hast passed the dolorous way before,
And we must follow where Thy steps have led.

Teach us to suffer meekly; Thou dost know
    The hidden wrong our contrite hearts confess,
    Thine eyes can read our deep unworthiness,
Thine ears are open to our cries of woe.

Help us to crush beneath our bleeding feet
    All base affections and all hopes unblest;
    The path of anguish leadeth on to rest,
We taste the bitter ere we touch the sweet.

Stray sunbeams wander through these darkened hours,
    And even in the solemn gloom of Lent
    Our chastened souls may feel a dim content,
Faint as the breath of springtide's pallid flowers.

Via Dolorosa

Then guide us till the mournful road is past;
    Though wet with tears, our faces learn to smile;
    Sorrow endureth for a little while,
But Easter light and joy shall come at last.

Good Friday Eve

Is it nothing to you, all ye that pass by? Behold and see if there be any sorrow like unto My sorrow.—LAMENTATIONS 1:12.

Will they think of Thy Cross and Thy sorrow,
    Thy pain that no mortal can know?
Will they watch for a few hours tomorrow
    With Thee in Thine infinite woe,
And turn from the world's crowded places
    Awhile with Thy people to be,
To kneel with the tears on their faces,
    And come in contrition to Thee?

Will they weep for the Heart that was broken
    That they might find comfort and bliss?
And oh, will they give Thee no token
    To show that they love Thee for this?
No sigh for the Brow that was bleeding,
    No tear for the spear-smitten Side!
Alas! will they pass on unheeding,
    As if no Redeemer had died?

O teach them with earnest endeavour
    To seek Thee while yet there is time;
Thy gates are not open for ever,
    Thy church-bells will ring their last chime:
That Voice full of soft invitation
    That pleads with the obdurate heart,
Hereafter in just indignation
    Shall say to the godless, "Depart."

Lord, show them Thine anguish tomorrow;
    And call unto those that pass by,
"Come, look on My passion and sorrow,
    And turn ye, for why will ye die?
I suffered, that ye might have pardon,
    I died, that your souls might be free,

I bled, for the hearts that ye harden;
  And will ye not come unto Me?"

Let us who have tasted Thy sweetness,
  Learn more of the depth of Thy woes;
For love is not love in completeness
  If sweetness is all that it knows;
It needeth the bitter to make it
  All perfect as love ought to be;
Then mix Thou the cup, Lord, we take it,
  And drink it tomorrow with Thee.

The Hardest Time of All

Hope deferred maketh the heart sick: but when the desire cometh,
it is as a tree of life.—PROVERBS 13:12.

There are days of silent sorrow
　　In the seasons of our life,
There are wild despairing moments,
　　There are hours of mental strife;
There are times of stony anguish,
　　When the tears refuse to fall;
But the waiting time, my brothers,
　　Is the hardest time of all.

Youth and love are oft impatient,
　　Seeking things beyond their reach;
And the heart grows sick of hoping
　　Ere it learns what life can teach:
For before the fruit be gathered
　　We must see the blossoms fall;
And the waiting time, my brothers,
　　Is the hardest time of all.

We can bear the heat of conflict,
　　Though the sudden crushing blow,
Beating back our gathered forces,
　　For a moment lays us low;
We may rise again beneath it,
　　None the weaker for the fall;
But the waiting time, my brothers,
　　Is the hardest time of all.

For it wears the eager spirit
　　As the salt waves wear the stone;
And the garb of hope grows threadbare,
　　Till the brightest tints are flown:
Then amid youth's radiant tresses
　　Silent snows begin to fall;
Oh, the waiting time, my brothers,
　　Is the hardest time of all!

But at last we learn the lesson
    That God knoweth what is best;
For with wisdom cometh patience,
    And of patience cometh rest;
Yea,—a golden thread is shining
    Through the tangled woof of fate;
And our hearts shall thank Him meekly,
    That He taught us how to wait.

An Autumn Message

"In the multitude of the sorrows that I had in my heart, Thy comforts have refreshed my soul."

In the dreamy autumn sunlight sleep the dim hills far away,
And softly shines the silver mist across the fields today;
The sweet-brier flaunts its scarlet now, and droops the laden vine,
And pearly jasmine-blossoms scent this quiet room of mine.

They are falling, ever falling, those pale stars so purely white,
They strew the level sward around like little flakes of light;
A breeze comes up this morning, and it freshens from the sea,
And drifting through the casement, whispers tenderly to me.

O the breeze—where has it wandered ere it sought my chamber here?
Does it come to bring a message from the scenes I hold so dear?
Has it passed an ancient city where the early morning air
Is hallowed by the church-bells ringing out the call to prayer?

While slowly through the solemn church the virgin sunbeams crept,
Perchance along those stately aisles the sighing zephyr swept,
And whispered near the windows where the burning colours fell
On the saintly sculptured faces with a beauty none can tell.

I am here amid the dropping leaves and fading Autumn flowers,
While steals the chilly twilight through the wan October bowers;
But the lilies keep their lustre on those sacred chancel panes,
And the sanctuary's glory is a light that never wanes.

The breeze has gone: it strayed away, along the dingle side;
It crept among the braken there, and laid it down and died:
The day's first prime is over, but the bees are booming yet
Round the fuchsia's waxen petals, and the beds of mignonette.

When the snowflakes hide my garden, and the cottage porch is bare,
And mine eyes are seeking vainly for the wealth of foliage there,
I can picture all the beauty in a land beyond my gaze,
And my spirit, looking upward, will not mourn for summer days!

An Autumn Message

And it may be that a breeze will come as it hath come today
With a message and a token from that city far away;
With a murmur of the music from the ancient church I love,
Drifting softly through my fancy like the low notes of a dove.

There will come another message, but I may not know the time,
Whether it shall be at even, or at morning's early prime;
It will reach me from a City that hath streets of purest gold,
Where the gates of pearl stand open, and the treasures are untold.

There the bliss is never ended, and the song is never done,
There the silver wings of angels shine around the Holy One;
And the white robes of the ransomed gleam beside the crystal sea:—
Should I turn aside or tremble, when that message comes to me?

The Father's Guidance

"He shall convert my soul, and bring me forth in the paths of righteousness for His name's sake."

I dared not trust my wayward will,
    I had no earthly guide;
In doubt and bitter loneliness
    For help and strength I cried;
And Thou wert near—an answer came
    To soothe my troubled breast;
I trusted in Thy worthy Name,
    And Thou hast brought me rest.

I do not ask a smoother way,
    From thorns and dangers free;
It is enough if I retain
    My fellowship with Thee:
I cannot wander while Thy hand
    So firmly claspeth mine,
And through a dry and barren land
    Thy streams of mercy shine.

Thy comforts have refreshed my soul,
    Thy sunshine gilds my way;
In weakness and in weariness
    Thy promise is my stay;
The secret sorrows of my heart
    To Thee are fully known;
Yea, though the joys of life depart
    I cannot feel alone.

And if I toil while others dream
    And sow while others reap,
O teach me for Thy blessed sake
    To weep with those that weep!
Teach me in faith and lowliness
    Some loving word to say;
Or drop some little flower to bless
    The mourner's rugged way.

The Father's Guidance

The deeds that He would have me do
   Are wrought by love and prayer;
A world of lowly charities
   Awaits His servant's care;
I need not seek some high emprise,
   Or lofty work for God,
While crowds of simple duties rise
   Like daisies from the sod.

With gentle hand He leads me on;—
   The shadows longer grow,
And softly o'er "the hills of time"
   I feel the night-winds blow;
Why should I tremble, when I see
   That valley, hushed and dim?
His rod and staff shall comfort me,
   And I am safe with Him.

Storm and Calm

I was glad when they said unto me, We will go into the house of the Lord.—PSALM 122:1.

The day had opened with a storm of showers,
    And winds awoke to greet that Sunday morn;
The garden-walks were strewn with broken flowers
    And scattered petals from the roses torn.

Scarlet and gold and purple blossoms lay
    All drenched and deadened by the blinding rain;
I knew that when the tempest passed away,
    Their ruined beauty could not bloom again.

Sometimes athwart the furrowed autumn slopes,
    A sea-gull, driven inland, flashed along;
But all the fields were dark as blighted hopes,
    And all the woods were void of choral song.

Yet as the day wore on, that leaden sky
    Showed rifts of silver gleaming here and there;
The loud wind sank into a sobbing sigh,
    And sweetly chimed the bells for evening prayer.

A stormy sunset—and the wild red light
    Flushed the grey, ivied tower with crimson glow;
Long golden rays of glory, dazzling bright,
    Slanted across the mossy graves below.

In the old church the solemn organ strain
    Like a deep voice through troubled bosoms thrilled;
Ah, who can tell what throbs of hidden pain
    Those blessed melodies have soothed and stilled!

How sweet the calm within His temple seemed
    After the tumult of that dreary day!
How tenderly the waning daylight beamed
    On lofty arch and ancient column grey!

Storm and Calm

Without—the misty landscape bathed in tears,
    The pale, wet blossoms clinging to the sod;
Within—the sacred harmony that cheers
    The Christian spirit with the peace of God!

Thus, Father, let us ever seek Thy rest
    In times of weariness and bitter woe;
Finding a shelter in Thy loving breast
    When grief has laid our brightest treasures low.

Teach us by faith to lift our thoughts above
    The ruined joys that strew these earthly ways;
Until we lose all sorrow in Thy love,
    And change our minor notes to songs of praise.

The Foolish Virgins

While the bridegroom tarried, they all slumbered and slept.
—Matthew 25:5.

When will the Bridegroom come? The birds are waking
 The budding forests from their long repose:
And through dark clods, the tender snowdrop breaking,
  Her pallid bosom shows.

O sisters, must our lamps be ever burning?
 Our eyes are weary, and our hopes decline;
Long have we waited for the Lord's returning,
  And yet He sends no sign.

Still onward glide the days:—a sound of sighing
 Makes mournful music in the boughs o'erhead;
And heaps of brown and amber leaves are lying
  About the path we tread.

Why comes He not? O friends, His promise faileth!
 Let us lie down awhile, and take our rest,
Lulled by this melancholy wind that waileth
  Over earth's faded breast.

The day has died away;—our lamps grow dimmer,
 Fresh oil shall feed them when tomorrow's light
Illumes the east;—and see, their feeble glimmer
  Will last throughout the night.

Rest, sisters, for your eyes are slumber-laden,
 Why should ye pause awhile your lamps to trim?
The Bridegroom comes not yet;—each weary maiden
  May sleep, and dream of Him.

Awake! awake! Through midnight stillness ringing
 Comes the sharp echo of that sudden cry!
Rise, virgins;—hear the herald angels singing,
  "The Bridegroom draweth nigh."

The Foolish Virgins

Ah, woe for us! Our last faint sparks are dying,
　　And nearer, nearer sounds that warning shout;
O give us oil—sweet sisters, hear our crying—
　　Help, for our lamps go out!

Hear us, the sadness of your glance appalleth!
　　O friends, have ye not known and loved us well?
Like drops of icy rain that answer falleth—
　　"Go ye to them that sell."

The door is shut;—yet He is full of kindness,
　　His tender love will pardon human sin:
The Bridegroom hath compassion on our blindness,
　　And He will let us in.

Lord, open unto us;—O King, receive us,
　　Our deep unworthiness and guilt we own;
Thou art so merciful, Thou wilt not leave us
　　In this dark night alone.

He speaks,—that solemn voice so calm and holy,
　　Its tone of ancient pity hath forgot;
Upon our souls the awful truth dawns slowly—
　　Lost—*for He knows us not!*

The Baptism of Suffering

Beloved, think it not strange concerning the fiery trial which is to try you, as though some strange thing happened unto you: But rejoice, inasmuch as ye are partakers of Christ's sufferings; that, when His glory shall be revealed, ye may be glad also with exceeding joy.—1 PETER 4:12–13.

If thou hast known some parting worse than death,
    The breaking of a tie that was thine all;
A pang that left thee hopeless—when thy breath
    Came slowly, and thy tears refused to fall;
Come in thy bitterness and gloom, and see
The moonlit Garden where He wept for thee.

If thou art stricken for His blessed sake
    Who bare for thee the scourge's cruel sting,
Rejoice, thy Lord hath called thee to partake
    Of His own baptism of suffering;
Low in that olive-shade He bowed for thee;
Bear on—remembering Gethsemane.

Bear on—for He hath loved thee, and thy tears
    Shall change to gems, and glitter on thy brow
In the calm light of the eternal years;
    And thy worn soul, so chafed and fettered now,
Shall know the freedom that He won for thee
    In the lone shadows of Gethsemane.

Confirmation Hymn

I will pay my vows unto the Lord, in the sight of all His people, in the courts of the Lord's house.—Psalm 116:18, 19.

Come in all reverence and deep contrition,
   Subdued by memories of youthful sin,
Kneel at His throne in lowliest submission,
   And with this day the better life begin.

Come with sweet thoughts of Jesus, and in meekness
   Take up the cross, and follow in His way;
His strength shall be made perfect in your weakness,
   His grace shall be your comfort and your stay.

Renew your vows—and seek His mercy only,
   To arm the trembling spirit for the strife;
Ye shall not fight the world's great battle lonely,
   Soldiers of Christ, ye bear a charmèd life.

Come, and the Holy Dove each promise sealing
   Shall fill your hearts and minds with pure desire;
Yea, while ye kneel, in humble prayer appealing,
   His gifts descend like Pentecostal fire.

And ever when the sacred rite is ended,
   Ye will have need of Jesus on your way;
Need of His love and watchful guidance blended,
   To keep the precious strength ye gain today.

Tender and clear as stars at even burning
   In dusky winter skies from east to west,
So shall ye shine—that all, your light discerning,
   May long to share that brightness calm and blest.

Sunday Morning Hymn

"The voice of praise and thanksgiving among such as keep holy day."

Day of holy recollections,
    Memories of praise and prayer,
Stirring all our deep affections,
    Hushing thoughts of worldly care;
Coming like the breath of summer
    Stealing over wintry lands,
Lifting up the weary spirit,
    Strengthening the feeble hands.

Day of peace—such depths revealing
    Of the love of Christ our King;
Day of rest—what balm of healing
    Can thy hallowed moments bring!
Foretaste of the bliss eternal
    That His ransomed ones shall know,
Blessed gift of consolation
    To His waiting church below.

In Thy sunlight seeing clearer
    Glimpses of the land of love,
By Thy worship drawing nearer
    To the sinless souls above,
Purified and soothed, and raisèd
    From earth's sordid mire and clay,
Evermore our hearts adore Thee
    For Thy hallowed seventh day!

We Thy pilgrims, fainting, fasting,
    Seek of Thee Thy living bread;
By Thy bounty everlasting
    Let the gracious food be spread;
fill the chalice of salvation
    From that crimson Fount of Thine;
Clothe us in the marriage-garment
    Ere we taste the feast divine.

Sunday Morning Hymn

From these blessed hours we borrow
    Music that shall linger long,
And the labours of tomorrow
    Shall be cheered by holy song;
Followed still by chanting voices,
    We may tread life's rugged way,
Ever in our hearts repeating
    Anthems that we sing today.

Alleluia! Lord of heaven,
    Throned in Triune majesty!
On this day of all the seven
    Sweetest hymns shall rise to Thee!
Alleluia! King of glory,
    Giver of all gifts of grace,
Let our humble praise ascending,
    Reach Thee in Thy holy place.

Sunday Evening Hymn

"Have I not remembered Thee in my bed, and thought upon Thee when I was waking?"

Now that our holy day is done,
    Our day so blest and bright,
Lord, for the sake of Thy dear Son,
    Vouchsafe us rest tonight.

Put thoughts of worldly strife aside,
    Let love and faith increase;
Grant us, on this calm eventide,
    Thine own best gift of peace.

Faint echoes of our sacred songs
    Shall haunt each weary brain,
Even in sleep the heart prolongs
    Our holy Sabbath strain.

And in our busy waking hours,
    O Father, still we pray,
Let music from immortal bowers
    Lighten the toils of day.

Send down through all the jars of time
    Some undertone of love,
A message from Thy sinless clime
    Of perfect bliss above.

Such songs shall help us to endure
    The world's discordant strife,
And keep our spirits calm and pure
    Amid the cares of life.

Until this earthly conflict cease,
    Lord, let us faithful be;
Thou wilt keep him in perfect peace
    Whose mind is stayed on Thee.

Alleluia

Ye are come unto Mount Sion, and unto the city of the living God, the heavenly Jerusalem, and to an innumerable company of angels.—HEBREWS 12:22.

Land of peace, and love, and brightness,
    Earthly spirits pine for thee!
Longing for those blessed regions
    Where all fettered hearts are free;
       Alleluia, Alleluia!
Sing Thy white-robed company.

Endless glory shineth in thee,
    For thy sun can never wane;
On thy gleaming, golden pavement,
    Walk the holy angel train;
       Alleluia, Alleluia!
Rolls the everlasting strain.

Golden harps and saintly voices
    All their hallowed music pour;
While thy ransomed sons and daughters
    Their Redeemers name adore;
       Alleluia, Alleluia!
Sing thy children evermore.

With the deep harmonious anthem
    Blends no mournful minor tone,
To the citizens of heaven
    Sighs and tears are never known;
       Alleluia, Alleluia!
Echoes round the great White Throne.

Lead us, O thou gentle Saviour,
    Upward to that holy place;
Washed, and ransomed, and forgiven
    By Thy wondrous work of grace;
       Alleluia, Alleluia!
We shall sing before Thy face.

Heart of Jesus, Pierced for Me

He shall see of the travail of His soul, and shall be satisfied.
—Isaiah 53:11.

Heart of Jesus, pierced for me,
Let my heart find rest in Thee;
Stream of pardon—tide of grace,
Purge away each sinful trace;
Let that flood celestial, flow
Till my soul is white as snow.
Riven Heart, O let me be
Sheltered, cleansed, and blest in Thee!

Arms of Jesus, stretched for me
On the Cross in agony,
Fold me in a sure embrace,
Hold me by the might of grace,
Make me steadfast in the fight,
Keep me from all false delight;
Clasp me close, until I stand
Safe within the better land.

Voice of Jesus, once for me
Raised in tones of misery,
When the bitter cry went up,
"Father, take away this cup!"
Soothe me in my dark distress,
Warn me in my heedlessness;
Plead for me, O Voice divine,
Blend my feeble prayers with Thine.

Love of Jesus, set on me,
Seeing all that was to be,
Knowing all the shame and scorn
That should meet the Virgin-born;
Love, that never sank or failed
When the powers of sin prevailed—
Fill my heart,—and let me be
Satisfied alone with Thee.

For All Thy Care We Bless Thee

Sing ye praises with understanding.—PSALM 47:7.

For all Thy care we bless Thee,
   O Father, God of might!
For golden hours of morning,
   And quiet hours of night:
Thine is the arm that shields us
   When danger threatens nigh,
And Thine the hand that yields us
   Rich gifts of earth and sky.

For all Thy love we bless Thee;
   No mortal lips can speak
Thy comfort to the weary,
   Thy pity for the weak:
By Thee life's path is brightened
   With sunshine and with song;
The heavy loads are lightened,
   The feeble hearts made strong.

For all Thy peace we bless Thee,
   That peace that spreads so wide;
The gracious benediction
   That falls upon Thy Bride;
For quiet meditation
   In days of prayer and fast,
For holy jubilation
   When Lenten shades are past.

For all Thy grace we bless Thee,
   That grace so full and free;
The banquet of salvation
   So richly spread by Thee;
When soul and body falter,
   And faith hath languid grown,
We know "we have an Altar"
   Where Thou wilt meet Thine own.

For all Thy truth we bless Thee;
    Our human vows are frail,
But through the strife of ages
    Thy word can never fail:
The kingdoms shall be broken,
    The mighty ones will fall,
The promise Thou hast spoken
    Shall triumph over all.

For all Thy saints we bless Thee,
    Our dearest ones who trod
The dark and thorny pathway
    That led them home to God;
For all who follow slowly
    The Master's toilsome way,
The brave, the pure, the lowly,
    Who strive, and watch, and pray.

For Thine own Church we bless Thee,
    Thy Spouse, our Mother dear;
O grant her strength and wisdom
    To keep her vigil here!
The watch is sad and weary,
    The Bridegroom tarries long;
But soon her "Miserere"
    Shall change to festal song!

O teach us how to praise Thee,
    And touch our lips with fire!
Yea, let Thy Dove descending,
    Our hearts and minds inspire;
Thus toiling, watching, singing,
    We tread our desert way,
And every hour is bringing
    Nearer, the dawn of day.

Hymns for Children – I

The vineyard which Thy right hand hath planted.—Psalm 80:15.

He hath gone into His garden
　To cull His flowerets fair;
And many a tender blossom
　Is blooming sweetly there.
He feeds among the lilies,
　He banquets on the vine;
He sends the soft south breezes,
　And bids His sunlight shine.

Are we within that garden?
　Are we among that band,
The flowers of His affection
　That bloom beneath His hand?
Lord Jesus, there enclose us,
　And let us thrive and grow;
The fruit of Thy fair vineyard,
　Thy lilies white as snow.

He hath gone into His garden,
　His sacred walls enclose
The cedar and the sapling,
　The rose-bud and the rose:
And not a bud can perish,
　And not a leaf can fall
Within the Saviour's garden,
　Because He loveth all.

He numbers all His blossoms;
　The smallest flowers must be
As precious to the Master
　As palm or cedar tree;
With watchful care He seeks them,
　In noontide or in shade;
And silver showers fall softly
　To freshen those that fade.

He comes to gather lilies;
    We may not know the hour
That makes some earthly blossom
    A bright immortal flower:
Then, Lord, may we be ready
    And waiting for Thy hand,
That we may bloom in glory
    In Thine eternal land.

Hymns for Children – II

A garden enclosed is my sister, my spouse.—SONG OF SOLOMON 4:12.

In Thy holy garden ground,
Jesus, let us all be found;
Bid that soft south wind of Thine
Breathe upon the tender vine,
Let Thine angel-guards, we pray,
Scare the hungry birds away:
Watch the soil where Thou hast sown,
Till Thy precious plants are grown.

Touched by Thine all-powerful hand
Let the little buds expand;
Bid the folded leaves unveil
Fragrant blossoms fair and pale;
Master, may Thy lilies grow
White and pure as driven snow,
Let Thy gracious dew and rain
Cleanse the flowers from earthly stain.

In Thy holy garden ground
If one drooping bough be found,
Spare the life which Thou didst give,
Bid the dying member live;
Lift it from the miry sod
Nearer to the skies of God,
Till it flourish, strong and free,
In its beauty praising Thee.

Fence Thy holy garden ground
From the wilderness around;
Chase the serpent from its bowers,
Guard Thine own beloved flowers;
Let no tainted breath creep in
From the poisoned haunts of sin;
Keep them from the world apart,
Make them pure, as pure Thou art.

Holy Communion – Hymn I

Verily, verily, I say unto you, Except ye eat the flesh of the Son of man, and drink His blood, ye have no life in you.—JOHN 6:53.

O comforter divine,
Come to this heart of mine,
Come and prepare my dear Redeemer's dwelling;
From Thy white wings outspread,
Let hope and peace be shed,
All vain and troubled thoughts and cares expelling.

Show me each secret sin
That lies so deep within,
Stifling with poisoned breath all pure emotion;
Let sighs of earnest prayer
Clear all the tainted air,
Till it grows odorous with true devotion.

Jesus, I humbly pray,
Enter my soul today,
In Bread and Wine Thyself to me revealing;
Lord, make me all Thine own,
Filled with Thy love alone,
Dead to the world and every sinful feeling.

Jesus, I humbly pray
That Thou wilt take away
The earth-born mists wherewith my faith is shrouded;
Here let me see Thy face,
In this Thy dwelling-place;
Shine on me, Saviour, in Thy light unclouded.

Come, Jesus, and restore
Each waning grace once more,
And let me taste Thee in the cup of blessing;
Pour from Thy heart to mine
Thy precious blood divine;
Let me go hence, the Life of life possessing.

Holy Communion – Hymn I

Feed me with living bread,
Let me be comforted
With the eternal food that cannot perish;
And when the Feast is done,
Rest with me, Holy One,
And teach me how Thy heavenly grace to cherish.

Holy Communion – Hymn II

Labour not for the meat which perisheth, but for that meat which endureth unto everlasting life, which the Son of man shall give unto you: for Him hath God the Father sealed.—JOHN 6:27.

Lay down thy burden for a little space,
And taste the fullness of thy Saviour's grace;
Come, for this Feast supplies thy deepest need,
His Flesh and Blood are meat and drink indeed.

Here, from thy dear Redeemer's heart to thine
Flows the life-giving stream in crimson wine:
Here in the bread, thy hungry soul may take
His sacred Body, given for thy sake.

Filled with His strength, thy spirit shall be strong
To fight against the foes that do thee wrong;
A purer Life within thy life shall lie,
Giving thee grace to win the victory.

This heavenly food shall help thee to sustain
Life's weary load of bitterness and pain;
The precious banquet He prepares today,
Keeps thee from fainting in the narrow way.

Come, thirsty soul, the cup is never dry,
His blood still flows this chalice to supply;
Come, famished heart, behold His table spread!
Himself the Feast, the everlasting Bread.

Come, and thy doubts and fears shall all subside
In the dear presence of the Crucified;
Come, and the company of heaven above
Shall join thee in this mystery of love.

With angels and archangels thou shalt feel
The joy that only Jesus can reveal;
With angels and archangels thou shalt raise
The Eucharistic strain of fervent praise.

Holy Communion – Hymn III

Ask, and it shall be given you; seek, and ye shall find—MAT. 7:7.

Shine through the mists of earth today,
    O face of Christ, unchanged, divine!
Meet me at Thine own feast, I pray,
    Draw near, O soul of Christ, to mine!

Once Thou wert bruisèd for my sake,
    O living Manna from on high!
Grant me with humble heart to take
    The food that still can satisfy.

O Rock of Israel! smitten sore
    Once in the wilderness for me;
Here would I drink, and thirst no more,
    Of that pure tide that flowed from Thee.

¹And still that blended stream imparts
    Its precious power to heal and bless;
The Blood, to pardon contrite hearts,
    The Water, bringing holiness.

Pardon and purity I need
    To cleanse me from my sinful stain,
Lord Jesus, teach me how to plead,
    And let no cry ascend in vain.

In lowly penitence I seek
    The grace and strength that in Thee dwell;
My faith is faint, my prayers are weak,
    But all my want Thou knowest well.

Thine is the glory, mine the night,
    Mine is the strife, and Thine the rest;
Shine on my darkness, Light of light,
    And lead the weary to Thy breast.

---

1 "As the Blood which He shed satisfied the Divine Justice, and removed our punishment, so the water washes and cleanses the pardoned soul; and both these blessings are inseparable, even as the Blood and water which flowed together out of His side."—JOHN AND CHARLES WESLEY.

Harvest Hymn – I

Be thankful unto Him, and speak good of His name.—PSALM 100:4.

Praise to the Father, praise
For blessings freely poured;
Praise for the golden harvest days,
And garners richly stored.

Praise Him for all His care,
For love that cannot cease;
For joys that rich and poor may share,
For plenty and for peace.

Praise to the Hand that made
The valleys thick with corn;
From breezy hill and quiet glade
The grateful strains are borne.

But let a deeper tone
With all our anthems blend;
Not for these earthly gifts alone
Should songs of praise ascend;

Praise for the living Bread
Descended from above;
Lord, let our empty souls be fed
At Thy great feast of love!

Christ, for Thy Church's sake,
Thy Body Thou didst give;
O grant us grace Thy bread to take,
That we may eat and live.

Enter each heart, we pray,
Supply our deepest need;
And make Thy sacred Flesh today
Our Bread of life indeed!

Harvest Hymn – II

"Yea, a joyful and pleasant thing it is to be thankful."

Lord of the golden harvest,
　　To Thee our songs we raise;
With endless adoration
　　We offer grateful praise.
Again our barns are teeming
　　With piles of ripened sheaves;
Again the mellow Autumn
　　Her fruitful garland weaves.

From purple-crested mountains,
　　From valleys green and low,
The strains of high thanksgiving
　　From happy hearts shall flow;
And joyful choirs shall praise Thee
　　Within Thy holy walls,
While like the dew from heaven
　　Thy benediction falls.

O Thou whose love hath given
　　These bounties of Thy grace,
Come to the hearts that seek Thee,
　　In this Thy dwelling-place.
Let hungry souls be strengthened
　　To bear earth's weary strife,
With Bread so freely broken,
　　And Wine of deathless life.

Watch Thou Thy faithful children
　　In this wide world of care,
For seeds of life eternal
　　The soil Thyself prepare;
The good grain sown in weakness
　　Upraised in power shall be,
The sowers and the reapers
　　Shall yet rejoice with Thee.

O God of life and glory,
　In that triumphal day
When all Thy wheat is gathered,
　And tares are swept away;
Within Thy blessed garner
　May we be safely stored,
The fruits of Christ's redemption,
　The harvest of the Lord!

To Father, Son, and Spirit,
　Our thankful songs are due,
We magnify and bless Thee,
　With love and homage true;
Our everlasting gladness
　From Thy great mercy springs,
Lord of the golden harvest,
　We hail Thee, King of kings!

Our Latter Days

A cloudy morning and a golden eve
    Warm with the glow that never lingers long;
Such is our life; and who would pause to grieve
    Over a tearful day that ends in song?

The dawn was grey, and dim with mist and rain;
    There was no sweetness in the chilly blast;
Dead leaves were strewn along the dusky lane
    That led us to the sunset light at last.

'Tis an old tale, beloved; we may find
    Heart-stories all around us just the same.
Speak to the sad, and tell them God is kind:
    Do they not tread the path through which *we* came?

Our youth went by in recklessness and haste,
    And precious things were lost as soon as gained;
Yet patiently our Father saw the waste,
    And gathered up the fragments that remained.

Taught by his love, we learnt to love aright;
    Led by his hand, we passed through dreary ways;
And now how lovely is the mellow light
    That shines so calmly on our latter days!

Children of the Sun

Dark hours!—Their shade was swiftly cast
   Where best we loved to roam;
Hours, when the voice of every blast
   Sighed of a vanished home.

Dark hours!—When God seemed far away,
   And all the world was chill;
But hearts that lacked the strength to pray
   Could wait to know His will.

And tenderly His love was shown;
   When joys died one by one
We found in paths we had not known
   The children of the sun—

The crocus, springing at our feet
   In dim and wintry days,
The sunflower, burning through the heat
   In radiant summer's ways.

Flowers of the sunshine and the sod!
   They sing an ancient song,
And tell us that the smile of God
   Is never hidden long.

No newer faith and hope they teach
   To lift the soul above;
For he who longs the sky to reach
   Must learn on earth of love.

The Watcher at the Gate

It was long ago that the children played
  In the quiet field where the daisies grew;
They twined the flowers, and the wreaths they made
  Were left all night in the summer dew;
"Oh, wait till the gold has died away,
  And a star shines over the old oak tree!"
But a soft voice answered—"I must not stay,
  For mother will watch at the gate for me."

The years went by, and I played no more
  In the daisied grass when the evening fell;
The heart, so light in the days of yore,
  Was burdened by griefs I could not tell;
But hope could quicken the weary feet
  That toiled through the twilight across the lea;
"I must hasten home," (oh, the thought was sweet!)
  "For mother will watch at the gate for me."

And now, when the long day's work is done,
  I go my way through the street or mart
In the loneliness that is known to One
  Who sees the depths of the mourning heart;
But angels come at the close of day,
  And sweet is the message they bear to me:
"Thou art near the end of the thorny way,
  And thy mother waits at the gate for thee."

Summer

Summer is come; we wake, and hear her singing
    Over the valleys thick with gold and green,
In lonely ways we feel her tendrils clinging
    Where only thorns have been.

Summer is come, and all the wild waste places
    With buds and leaves and blossoms overflow;
Ten thousand rainbow dyes, ten thousand graces
    Arise, and bloom, and glow.

What hast thou brought us but these glories shining,
    O summer, through thy few bright golden hours?
Can hearts that ache with life's unspoken pining
    Be filled with song and flowers?

Ah no; we wait, we wait for fuller sweetness,
    For love, made holy by the sorrow past,
For a new life in all its fair completeness,
    Our hope fulfilled at last.

And when the soul this narrow world forsaking
    Gains the full splendour of eternal day,
Summer shall come with that sublime awaking,
    And shadows flee away.

A Little While Ago

It was only a little while ago;
The sun went down and the tide was low;
And the light that lies on the rock-strewn shore
Is always sweet when the day is o'er;
Tender and calm to the weary men,
But never so fair as it seemed just then,
For it shone in the face I loved the best,
And you promised a home of peace and rest.

It was only a little while ago,
The sea was bright with an amber glow;
Away to the west the ocean rolled,
And lost itself in a mist of gold;
And all the years of our life to be
Were veiled in light like that shining sea;
Alas! for the human eyes that fail
To see the sorrow behind the veil!

A little while—and the darkness fell,
With a gloom and anguish no words can tell;
Your soul went out, when the tide was low,
To the world of love that we may not know;
Do you still remember, far off or near,
The faithful heart that is waiting here?
When the morning breaks, and the shadows flee
And the pain is past, will you come for me?

From Peace to Rest

There is a sleep that the children know,
A hush that comes with the sunset glow,
When the dimpled limbs are laid to rest,
And the bright eyes close on a loving breast;
And the happy fancy, tired of play,
Goes off to a dreamland far away:
The fathers wake and the mothers weep
When times are hard; but the children sleep.

There is a rest that the saints shall know
While the crowds around them come and go;
When the bonds shall break, and the soul be free
To seek those joys that we may not see;
And we, who stand by the lifeless clay,
What know we yet of the spirit's way?
We cannot follow that upward flight
From the gloom of earth to the realms of light.

O Father, here in Thy world below
Let heaven begin in the lives we know;
In the weary brain and the troubled breast
Let there be quiet and love and rest;
So pain and patience, and toil and strife
Shall serve to cherish the higher life,
Till the bonds shall break and the conflict cease,
And we pass in silence from peace to peace.

On the Threshold of the Year

On the threshold of the year,
Ere the snow-wreaths disappear,
Half in hope and half in fear,
    Waits the heart;
When the coming days are sweet,
And the buds blow round our feet,
In the pathway, who will meet?
    Who will part?

When the daffodils expand,
And the sun is on the land,
Some will travel hand in hand,
    Calm and blest;
When the meadows wear their gold,
And the lily-bells unfold,
Underneath the daisied mould
    Some will rest.

On the threshold of the year,
See, the Lord is standing near,
And the heart forgets its fear
    In His smile;
Trembling soul, He speaks to thee,
"I, myself, thy guide will be—
All the way is known to Me,
    Mile by mile.

"On the threshold of the year,
If the path looks dim and drear,
Then My love shall make it clear
    To thine eyes;
Only trust thy changeless Friend,
If thou wilt on Me depend,
What awaits thee at the end?
    Paradise!"

The River's Song

The voice of the river is sweet and strong,
It sings to the rushes an old, old song.

The wind is fickle, and varies its tone,
Sometimes a whisper and sometimes a moan.

The leaves and the branches rustle and sway,
Changing their music ten times a day;

And the voice of a man is a voice of change,
Mirthful and passionate, loving and strange.

But be the day cloudy, or brief, or long,
The river will sing you the same old song.

'Tis a song of gladness, and rest, and hope,
Of a brighter life, and a wider scope;

Of narrowing channels and wild rocks past,
And the broad blue sea with its peace at last.

The Two Houses

My father's house stands under the hill,
A lowly cottage, serene and still;
The thatch is cushioned with green and gold,
The mouldering walls are grey and old.

Year after year, underneath the caves,
The starlings build in the ivy-leaves;
And up to the chimneys, brown and low,
The climbing sprays of the woodbine grow.

Within the walls there are love and trust—
Those treasures untouched by moth and rust;
But through the crannies the rain drip in,
And the daily bread is hard to win.

And the willing hands grow weak and fail,
The loving faces wax thin and pale;
The work is long, and the rest is brief,
And bright hopes fade like the autumn leaf.

And day by day, when we sleep or wake,
We know that the strongest links may break.
My father's house is a house of care,
Though faithful hearts are abiding there.

My Father's house on the hill-top stands,
Above the valleys and pasture lands;
The light of the sunrise softly falls
On green mounds sheltered beneath its walls.

Without there is toil, and pain, and loss;
Within the crown is above the cross;
Without the hungry that are not fed;
Within the manna, the Living Bread.

And here, with hope that can never die,
We hear of another house on high,

The Two Houses

Not made with hands, nor fashioned of clay,
Nor touched with the taint of earth's decay—

A home secure from sorrows and tears,
Where youth and strength shall outlast the years;
Where strife is over and woe shall cease,
And heart-throbs rest in eternal peace.

The soul grows weary of working days,
And tired of walking in troubled ways.
My Father's house is a house of prayer,
And faithful hearts find a refuge there.

A Prayer by the Sea

I saw the ships on a windy sea
    In the light of the morning's gold;
And the shout of the sailors came to me
    Like songs from the days of old.

Wild waves leaped up on the crags and beat
    On the edge of the rock-bound shore;
And the thought of a coming time was sweet,
    When the sea should be no more.

No more, no more shall mothers and wives
    Dream of loves that the blue wastes hide;
No more shall the vigorous hearts and lives
    Be flung to the wind and tide!

Oh, Father, follow the gallant ships
    Through the light of the morning pale!
Thou hearest the prayer of the loving lips,
    Thy mercy never can fail.

And guide us all to some haven blest
    Where never a tempest is known;
For life is sad, and the secret of rest
    Is hidden with Thee alone.

Christs Question

Then Jesus saith unto them, Children, have ye any meat?—JOHN 21:5.

"Children, have ye any meat?"
    Comes the question soft and low,
Like a breath of summer sweet,
    Stealing over wastes of snow.
All our needs the Saviour knew,
    Needs that He will not forget;
To His ancient kindness true,
    Human longings touch Him yet.

"Children, have ye any meat?"
    Winter days are hard and cold;
Wearily, from field and street,
    Comes the answer as of old.
Jesus, Master, Thou wert known
    Long ago in breaking bread:
Let Thy love through us be shown,
    And the hungry ones be fed.

"Children, have ye any meat?"
    Lord, we do Thy will today;
Eager lips Thy words repeat,
    None are empty sent away;
Birds, whose notes are full of praise,
    Share the bounties of Thine hand:
Ay, on dreary winter days
    There is gladness in the land.

"Children, have ye any meat?"
    (Deeper still the accents sound):
Christ, to famished souls how sweet
    Shall the bread of life be found!
From those plenteous stores of Thine
    Feed them in their daily race,
Till they drink Thine own new wine
    In the kingdom of Thy grace.

The Few

Out on the plains of the far-away West,
Some one who loved you has gone to his rest;
Under the bloom of the prairie he lies,
One of the few who are honest and wise;
One who was noble when others were base,
One who could look a false world in the face;
Out of your life dropped a soul that was true,
 One of the few.

Down in a village that nobody knows,
Some one is going "the way of the rose";
One who was constant through changes of lot,
One who remembered when others forgot;
Patient and tender, she clung to you fast,
In the dark days of your sorrowful past;
Out of your life fades a soul that is true,
 One of the few.

What is there left in the crowd that you seek?
Hearts that are shallow, and loveless, and weak;
Few are the Faithfuls in Vanity Fair,
Lover and friend are no sojourners there;
Angels pass by you with pitying eyes,
Follow their path-way wherever it lies;
Dare to be steadfast, and simple, and true,
 One of the few.

Longings

In mist and gloom the daylight swiftly dies,
    The city lamps shine out along the street;
No vesper glory charms the weary eyes,
    No leafy murmurs make the gloaming sweet.
"Ah me, the tranquil evening hours," she cried,
"Amid the rushes by the river-side!

"The busy feet for ever come and go,
    The sounds of work and strife are never still.
Oh, for the grassy pastures, green and low,
    The strawberry-blossom and the daffodil!
How peacefully the mellow sunshine died
Amid the rushes by the river-side!

"I loved the toil amid those reedy shades,
    At sunrise or at sunset, gay and light;
The song of waters and the laugh of maids
    Come back to me in happy dreams at night;
Oh, blessed hours, when free from care and pride
I bound the rushes by the river-side!

"This is no dwelling-place for hearts like mine,
    Hearts that are born for freedom and for rest.
Ah me, to see the marshy meadows shine
    In the low sunlight of the saffron west!
I will go home to find my peace," she cried,
"Amid the rushes by the river-side."

Night and Morning

Sorrow and storm upon the deep,
    Wild light, and thunder-roar!
The good ship laboured heavily
    A mile away from shore.
"Ah me, what will the morning bring?"
    I heard a woman cry;
"The waves are strong, the night is long,
    No helping hands are nigh!"
Oh, bitter, bitter was the wail
    Of wives upon the beach;
Love wrestled there in fervent prayer
    For those it could not reach.

Sorrow and sighing in the room
    Where lights were burning low;
A soul was called away from earth,
    And longed, yet feared to go,
For thoughts of bygone doubt and sin
    O'erwhelmed it like a tide,
And darkness lay across the way
    That leads to Life untried;
"Ah me, what will the morning bring?"
    I heard the watchers cry;
Love wrestled there in fervent prayer,
    But death was drawing nigh.

The day broke slowly, cool and grey
    And calm from east to west;
The ship was safe within the bay,
    The soul had gone to rest;
For God was greater than the wave,
    And stronger than the blast;
Oh, soul and bark, through storm and dark
    Ye came to *peace* at last!

On a Rock-Bound Coast

High on the rocky crest above the billows
    He sits alone, to dream
Of rush-grown banks and boughs of trailing willows
    Shading his native stream.

Ah me! amid the crash of ocean thunder
    Against the dark sea crags,
He hears the little brook go rippling under
    A screen of reeds and flags.

The sea-gull, soaring o'er these barren ledges,
    Utters her wailing cry;
But he can hear the mavis in the hedges
    Sing to the summer sky.

Oh, like the exile, ever fondly keeping
    Home-thoughts within his breast,
We pine for home, and dream, awake or sleeping,
    Of our "dear land of rest":

That better country, by no billows bounded,
    Where never storm shall be;
Sweet in our ears the Father's words have sounded—
    "There shall be no more sea."

No sea, no heart-wreck, no tempestuous heaving
    Of waves that still increase,
But endless calm with Him, in whom believing,
    We have eternal peace.

Demas

For I am now ready to be offered, and the time of my departure is at hand. For Demas hath forsaken me, having loved this present world.
                                                    —2 TIMOTHY 4:6, 10.

"I am ready to be offered;
        Ready, for the strife is done,
For the course on earth is finished,
        And the crown is nearly won;
Oft in weariness and weakness,
        Oft in peril of the sword,
Still I strove in faith and meekness,
        I, the prisoner of the Lord.
Come,[1] for autumn winds are wailing,
        And the spirit longs for thee;
Age is lonely, friends are failing,
        Demas hath forsaken me."

Thus the words of Paul the aged
        Echo down the aisles of time,
Telling of a trust unshaken,
        And a life that was sublime;
Only one soft note of grieving
        Through the triumph makes its way—
In the world that he was leaving
        One faint heart had gone astray;
Waiting for a glorious morrow,
        Soon his risen Lord to see,
Still he sighs, in human sorrow,
        "Demas hath forsaken me."

There are thankless souls, and faithless,
        Father, in this world of Thine,
From the Bread of Heaven turning
        To the husks that feed the swine;

---

1 Do thy diligence to come shortly unto me.—2 TIMOTHY 4:9.

And Thy servants, toiling, praying
    For the kingdom of Thy grace,
Weep to see these children straying
    Far away from Thy dear face;
Bring them back to paths of gladness,
    Let Thy Spirit strive for Thee,
Lest they hear Thee say in sadness,
    "Lo, ye have forsaken me!"

A Legend of the South Coast

It was the time of golden sheaves,
    When peasants toil the most;
And a knight came riding, under the leaves,
    Along the fair south coast.

Under the leaves of oak and beech,
    The good knight rode along;
And over the lea by the salt blue sea
    Came up the harvest song.

"O tarry now, my red-roan steed,
    Well hast thou played thy part;
There is rest for thee 'neath the green oak tree,
    And peace for my poor heart!

"For I have heard my reapers sing
    Along the fair south coast;
And a braver song I shall hear ere long
    Amid God's angel-host.

"And I have seen the blue waves shine
    Beneath the sun today,
But the Crystal Sea, it waiteth for me,
    Where harpers harp alway."

Along the lane a damsel strayed
    To pull the white bindweed,
And she was aware of a knight rode there
    Upon a red-roan steed.

The low sun glinted on his crest,
    His plume was red as wine,
And he bare the red-cross upon his breast
    That told of Palestine.

Upon the towers of Portchester
    The haze of sunset fell;

And the vesper chime of that olden time
    Rang from its grey chapelle.

Under the leaves of oak and beech
    The damsel knelt to pray;
Or ever she wist, in a golden mist
    The knight had passed away.

She took the red-roan charger's rein
    (A weary steed was he),
And led him straight to a castle gate
    That stood close by the sea.

A cry went o'er the harvest fields,
    "Peace to Sir Hugo's ghost!"
And they reaped his lands by the salt sea shore,
But they knew that the knight would ride no more
    Along the fair south coast.

When the Children Are at Rest

When the household cares are over,
  And the quiet zephyrs pass
Through the crimson heads of clover
  And the daisies in the grass;
Then the mother's busy fingers
  Do their silent labour best,
Toiling fast while daylight lingers
  And the children are at rest.

In the sunny hours of morning
  She had other work to do,
Softly chiding, gently warning,
  Watching all the noontide through;
Love and strife and pain and pleasure,
  Crowd within one little nest,
Mother hearts can find no leisure
  Till the children are at rest.

While we sleep the father waketh,
  Working, watching for us all,
In His mighty hands He taketh
  All the tasks that we let fall;
We have wrangled, toiled, and striven
  Through a long and weary day,
Lo! we rest, and help is given,
  And the pain is soothed away.

He who loves us will not slumber
  While our feeble hands are still,
Blessings that we cannot number
  All the hours of darkness fill,
Till the broken links are mended,
  And the worst becomes the best,
And the toilsome task is ended
  While His children are at rest.

Wondering

When autumn, with burnished fingers,
  Has gilded the wildwood bowers,
I wonder if Mabel lingers,
  Alone, in those haunts of ours.

Do memories, sweet and bitter,
  Come back when the night-wind sighs,
And only a few stars glitter
  In heaven, like watchful eyes?

Does Mabel ever remember
  A summer of shade and gleam,
And pine for an old September
  That passed in a golden dream?

I wonder, I often wonder,
  Why peace on her path should be,
While only the storm and thunder
  Of life are given to me.

I do not covet the sweetness
  She finds where the grass grows long—
The joy in her flower's completeness,
  The charm in her river's song.

But here, in the world's great Babel,
  Worn out with the strife and pain,
I wonder if little Mabel
  Is longing for me again.

God's love is too deep for guessing;
  He sees what we cannot know—
The grief that enshrines a blessing,
  The bliss that enfolds a woe.

The hearts that He keeps asunder
  Will meet in His own bright day;
So, Mabel, I cease to wonder:
  I wait, my darling, and pray.

The Voice of Many Waters

The voice of many waters,
    In valleys cool and dim,
Sings to the weary wayfarer
    A sweet eternal hymn:
For ever breaks the silver shower
    Upon the quiet sod,
And murmurs—"Glory, honour, power,
    Unto the Lord our God."

The voice of many waters
    Sings to the troubled soul,
Through all the loud world's busy ways
    Immortal anthems roll.
There is no silence in the heart
    God's music cannot fill;
There is no strife of crowd or mart
    His thunder cannot still.

The voice of many waters
    Bursts on the lonely way:
"Sing us the songs of Sion" cry
    The mourners day by day;
The wail of want, and pain, and wrong,
    Is heard on land and sea,
O Lord, how can we sing Thy song
    When we are far from Thee?

God of the living fountains
    And everlasting hills!
Thy name is graven on our hearts,
    Thy voice our being fills!
Oh, lead us through these weary years
    By paths we have not known,
Till Thou shalt wipe away all tears
    Before the Father's throne.

On the Cliff

Just where the sand is warm and bright,
    And strewn with shells today,
Bathed in the stainless morning light,
    In his last sleep he lay.

I think the angels watch the place
    And linger here with me,
And tell me I shall see his face
    Where there is no more sea.

I hear them come on quiet wings
    When all the earth is still.
God will reveal His hidden things
    To those that do His will.

I loved him with a woman's heart,
    Strong, passionate, and deep;
The love that lives its life apart,
    And wakes while others sleep.

And lighter spirits laughed and sung
    When boats put off from shore,
But I went in, with silent tongue,
    And shut the cabin door.

Only one little year has flown
    Since Lizzie's man went down,
But she no longer bears alone
    Her basket to the town.

And Nell has found another mate,
    And made another nest;
But in my empty house I wait
    Till God shall give me rest.

And often when the silver sails
    Glide out to meet the dawn,

On the Cliff

I say, "His promise never fails;
   His love is not withdrawn."

I, too, shall go to meet the day
   That knows no setting sun;
And my dark years shall fade away
   When the new home is won.

Summer Dreamers

A boy and a girl by the wide blue sea
    Sat close together, and whispered low;
He was a dreamer, and so was she,
    In the happy summers of long ago.
He meant to grow up so strong, so wise,
    That wealth and fame should come at his call;
She looked at him with her shining eyes,
    Smiled and believed it all!

A man and woman sat side by side
    One golden summer, when life was new;
His voice was soft as the quiet tide,
    And love, he said, should be always true;
She looked at him with her trustful eyes
    (The tears had gathered, ready to fall),
And, in her gladness and sweet surprise,
    Sighed—and believed it all!

The song of the summer wave is sweet,
    It seeks the sand with a tender kiss;
The girls sit on the sunny seat
    Listen, and dream of a world of bliss;
And He who has bound the waters fast,
    And even watches the sparrow's fall,
Knows every thought, and from first to last,
    Cares for these dreamers all.

A Wedding Hymn

Written for use in the Savoy Chapel Royal.

Thou who hast promised Thy children to guide,
Thou who dost cherish Thy mystical Bride,
Come with the blessing Thy chosen ones claim;
Blessed be these whom we bless in Thy name.

Bless them in loving, and teach them to be
True to each other and faithful to Thee;
Bless them in living, for life is more sweet
If all its treasures are poured at Thy feet.

Bless them in keeping the vow that they make,
Bless them in bearing the cross for Thy sake;
If the fine gold in the fire should be cast,
Let it shine bright when the trial is past.

Through the green pastures where waters are still,
Call them to follow Thee, doing Thy will;
In the dark valley Thy light may they see,
Darkness and light are alike unto Thee.

Father of all, many mansions are Thine,
Give them a place in Thy dwelling divine;
Sweet are the households of earth with their love,
Sweeter by far is Thy kingdom above!

"Mine Own Familiar Friend"

Old friend, kind friend, is the night far spent?
    As half in a dream I lie,
There comes the thrill of a sweet content
    That tells me a friend is nigh:
The forest rests in a waste of snow,
    In its wintry slumber deep;
But when spring awakes and violets blow,
    Then I shall be fast asleep.

Old friend, there were many false, fair things
    In that life of mine gone past:
The rosy blossom that breaks, and stings,
    And pierces the heart at last;
Bright smiles, that cover a love grown cold,
    The honey that turns to gall;
The tinsel purchased with honest gold—
    Ah, friend, I have known them all!

But one thing, one, through shadow and shine,
    Is true to the very end—
Of all good gifts that ever were mine
    The best is a faithful friend:
You saw the snares that I could not see,
    And watched me early and late;
My soul was dumb, but your hand, for me,
    Knocked hard at the Golden Gate.

Old friend, kind friend, is the night far spent?
    As half in a dream I lie,
I feel the calm of a deep content,
    And know that your God is nigh.
Now sleep a little, for I can rest,
    The dawn breaks over the snow;
Sleep—but the heart in your faithful breast
    Is ever waking, I know.

A Breath of Summer

The snow still lingered in the upland hollows,
　　And chilly daisies quivered at the blast;
Day after day we waited for the swallows,
　　And dreamed of kinder springs, and summers past.

One morn we heard the little finches singing;
　　And to the shepherd on the breezy brae
There came a wind across the ocean, bringing
　　The scent of bowers full-blossomed, far away.

Then earth rejoiced, and souls forgot their sorrow,
　　And cheerful sunbeams flashed on vale and hill;
And hope revived, and whispered that tomorrow
　　Would come with smiles, and be more lovely still.

Lord, when our lives are full of grief unspoken,
　　Worn with long weariness, oppressed with gloom
Grant us a breath of summer—send a token
　　From Thy sweet land of everlasting bloom!

Thou knowest all the doubt, the fear, the failing
　　Of feeble faith that cannot trust Thee long;
Father, forgive, and let Thy love prevailing
　　Teach the faint heart to know Thee and be strong.

Answers

Summer wind, let the hawthorns rest,
    Leave the blossom to deck the bough.
"Nay, I scatter them east and west—
    Who knows where they are drifting now?"

Gentle sea, let the white sails stay;
    Life is brief, and to part is pain.
"Nay, I carry them far away—
    Who knows when they may come again?"

Father Time, let the dreamer be;
    Spare the visions that charm my sleep.
"Nay, I laugh at thy dreams and thee;
    Thou shalt lose them, and wake to weep."

Wind, and billow, and ruthless Time,
    All your triumph shall soon be past!
I am bound for a fairer clime,
    Where lost treasures are found at last.

Blooms of summer, and loves of old,
    Hopes that faded and seemed to die,
Things more precious than gems or gold
    God has stored in His house on high.

After the Rain

After the rain, my friend,
   After the rain,
Soon will the Father send
   Gladness again;

Weeping endures a while,
   Joy comes at last,
Brighter the world shall smile
   When tears are past.

Far yonder cloud shall flee
   Over the height;
There, on the darkened sea,
   Fall gleams of light;

After the rain, my love,
   After the rain
Sunshine, like Noah's dove,
   Steals back again;

Brave souls can bear the showers,
   Heavy and chill,
Hearts that are strong as ours
   Grief cannot kill;

Wait, with your hand in mine.
   Trustful and true,
Wait, till the glories shine
   Out of the blue!

After the rain, my dear,
   After the rain
Skies will be calm and clear,
   Birds sing again;

Blossoms shall ope their eyes,
   Blooming and bright;

After the Rain

Earth will be paradise,
    Life a delight;

Only be hopeful, sweet,
    Never complain;
Daisies will kiss your feet,
    After the rain!

Restored

The dawn is breaking—open wide the shutter,
  Let in the salt breeze from the silver bay;
See how the leaves around the lattice flutter
  In the first breath of this sweet summer day!

And lying here, (your face beside my pillow,
  Your hand in mine,) I mark the shadows flee;
And catch the glory on some far-off billow,
  And feel the strange enchantment of the sea.

True friend, true love, your patient watch is ended;
  (It is of life, not death, yon skylark sings!)
At dead of night God's messenger descended,
  Silent and swift, with healing on his wings.

My heart awoke to passionate thanksgiving,
  As future years before my vision came;
The Lord has numbered me among the living,
  Blessed for ever be His holy name!

How freshly sweet this early wind is blowing,
  How fair the morning looks on sea and shore!
We shall go forth together, surely knowing
  That He will guide our steps for evermore.

Waiting by the Stream

Deep amid the scented grasses
    Where the waters glide and gleam,
Ere the vesper glory passes
    They are waiting by the stream.

And the south wind stirs the clover,
    And the blossoms bend and sigh;
For the summer day is over,
    And the golden time goes by.

Then he whispers that tomorrow
    Shall be sweeter than today;
But she answers, "Who can borrow
    What the river sweeps away?

"For the blooms have no abiding
    On the tendril or the tree,
They are falling—floating—gliding
    To the everlasting sea!"

When the gold is on the hedges,
    And the mist is like a dream,
Deep amid the nodding sedges
    He is waiting by the stream,

And the autumn lights are lying
    On the river and the shore;
But a lonely heart is sighing
    For the love that comes no more.

"Oh, my Father," he is pleading,
    "Let me follow her to Thee!"
But the tide goes on unheeding
    To the everlasting sea.

Yet a voice of benediction
    Speaks within the mourner's breast:
"On the waters of affliction
    I will bear thee safe to rest."

The Old Cottage

We knew that the walls were battered
    And let in the wind and the rain;
The children were gone and scattered,
    And never would come back again;
But the home seemed all the dearer
    For the signs of its swift decay,
And the past grows ever clearer
    When lives are wearing away.

We listen to baby voices
    And the patter of baby feet;
For the heart, grown old, rejoices
    In a life that was young and sweet;
Though the nest is left forsaken,
    The echoes of music abide;
And the joys that time has taken
    Are fairer than aught beside.

With grief that is past our telling,
    And hearts that are ready to break,
We mourn for the dear old dwelling—
    So dear for the little ones' sake;
And still, as the evenings darken,
    And clouds hang over the west,
Our souls are waking, to hearken
    For God to call us to rest.

Spring and the Heart

THE HEART SPEAKS

Bring me the gold of gorses from the hills;
    The blooms that cluster thick upon the thorn;
The marybuds that blow by meadow-rills;
    The clover, rosy as the blush of morn.

Scatter thy gifts, O Spring, with lavish hand,
    Thy precious gifts of sunlight, song, and dew!
Send the bird-voices thrilling through the land;
    Dress the bare woods in leafage green and new.

Call back the swallows to their haunts again;
    Bring the white sails across a placid sea;
Bid the young corn spring up in sun and rain,
    And let but one small joy arise for me!

For me—for I have lost so many things
    While the grim Winter reared his icy throne!
Old hopes, old dreams, the gleam of silver wings,
    Pass'd from my life, and left me dark and lone.

SPRING SPEAKS

To thee, poor heart, I come with empty hands,
    Mine are but blossoms born of sun and showers;
The hopes thou seekest grow not on my lands,
    And thy dead loves revive not with my flowers.

Turn thee to other souls, more sad than thine,
    Into their darkness bring the light of day;
Load them forth gently into paths divine,
    And thou shalt find a blessing on the way.

A blessing that shall live when daisies die;
    A bliss that fades not when the sere leaves fall;
A new joy, fairer than the joys gone by,
    And for its sake thou wilt forget them all.

Unforgotten

You think you are forgotten now,
    Old things have passed away;
As time goes on you wonder how
    I live from day to day.

Your name is never on my lip,
    But always in my prayer;
The blessings that your hand let slip
    I hoard with silent care.

Your good desires that came and went,
    Your tears that none might see,
Your feeble yearnings to repent—
    These things are stored with me;

Stored in that treasure-house of love
    That holds not gold nor gem,
Poor treasures;—yes, but One above
    Knows how to value them;

And when the life-cloud breaks apart,
    And severed spirits meet,
I will unlock my guarded heart
    And lay them at your feet.

The City Churchyard

In the great heart of the city, where the workers never sleep,
You may find an ancient graveyard full of shadows still and deep.

Here the birds build in the branches, and the small white daisies grow,
And the summer lights fall softly on the quiet stones below.

Loud and clear on Sunday mornings sound the bells along the street,
Till the heart wakes at their summons with desire and longing sweet.

Then a wave of organ-music sweeps across the pleasant sod,
And the worshippers are gathered in the time-worn house of God.

Strains of prayer and praise are flowing o'er the grave-stones old and grey,
Where the waiting dust is sleeping till the Resurrection Day.

And the living, worn with labour, linger here for calm and rest,
For of all good things the Father gives, the gift of peace is best.

From the churchyard comes the promise unto all who wake and weep,
After days of patient toil He giveth His beloved sleep.

Washed Ashore

Old Mike dwelt under the Curlew Cliff;
  The cliff is white as curds,
The sands beneath it are gold and grey,
And the long swell murmurs night and day
  Like music without words.

But a lonely soul was poor old Mike,
  And one whose heart was sore;
His little girl, with the golden head,
Went out in the world, the neighbours said,
  And she came back no more.

When the children built their towers of shells
  And laughed to see them fall,
The tide ran up to the sunny strand,
And chased the steps of the bright-eyed band,
  And old Mike loved them all.

For sorrow never can turn us sour,
  If God's love keeps us sweet;
And a wholesome heart may find its bliss
In a child's fresh laugh and dewy kiss
  As long as it shall beat.

But the blue sea does not always play
  With little ones on shore;
Sometimes it wakes with a giant's might,
And small waves swell to an awful height,
  And burst with angry roar.

A fickle friend is the grand old sea,
  Whose changes none can tell;
It rose one day in a cruel mood,
And roared as a lion roars for food,
  Just after twilight fell.

On the wild wild sands the fishers stood,
  And gazed through mist and storm;

The surf dashed high, and the light was dim,
But old Mike said there was shown to him
    A vessel's tossing form.

The others turned from the shore away;
    But he watched there alone,
And prayed for the souls in mortal pain,
Till the faint gray daylight crept again
    O'er cliff and sand and stone.

And just at the base of Curlew Cliff
    Lay something still and cold;
And the seaweed wrapped it round and round,
But Mike beheld, with a great heart-bound,
    Its dripping curls of gold.

"The ways of God are not ours," he said;
    "I thought Him hard to me;
The grave has taken my fairest things,
But lo! this day to my feet He brings
    A treasure from the sea."

"'Tis better to wait His time," he said,
    "Than win our way and will;
The plans of God are past finding out,
And we test His love with cry and doubt,
    But find it changeless still."

To his cabin, built beneath the cliff,
    The senseless child he bore,
And the eager folk came crowding down
From the scattered cots and busy town,
    To that rain-beaten shore.

Long, long it seemed ere her eyes unclosed,
    Long ere they heard her sigh;
On her neck and wrists were jewelled bands,
And Mike unclasped them with gentle hands,
    And laid them safely by.

And days went on, and her baby smile
   Lit up his cabin small,
Till his waste life blossomed like the rose;
The years that come at the journey's close
   Are often best of all.

And the neighbours called the maiden Pearl,
   So bright she grew, and fair;
An ocean gem, by the billows thrown
Into a casket, empty and lone,
   To shrine its beauty there.

When Mike lay calm in his dying hours
   She watched him night and day;
But a proud lord to the cabin came,
And called the girl by her mother's name,
   And bade her come away.

"I sought my daughter many a year"
   (He told her o'er and o'er);
"In a cruel storm my wife was lost;
But seamen spoke of a baby, toss'd
   On some unfriendly shore."

Then old Mike whispered, "I found the child,
   Washed up by yonder brine,
A pearl of price from the stormy sea;
Our God has lent her for years to me;
   Now take her, she is thine."

But Pearl looked up in her father's face,
   "Not yet, not yet," said she;
"There is time to give, and time to take,
I cling to him for his long love's sake,
   While he has need of me!"

On Two Sides

How calmly the day is fading,
   How softly the sunlights gleam!
Amid the shining and shading
   I think I begin to dream.

Now close the book, little Ethel,
   I want to ponder and wait;
This quiet room is a Bethel,
   And sorrow is heaven's gate.

I never thought of thanksgiving
   Till strength was taken away;
You knew that I went on living
   A life that was cold and gay.

I called you a foolish dreamer,
   A dweller in mist and cloud;
While I was the thoughtful schemer,
   Too wise for the common crowd!

And yet, through my fast-shut portal
   The tone of your voice came faint;
Your song was a song immortal,
   Your face the face of a saint.

In silence you saw me wreathing
   My brow with a laurel crowns;
But yours were the violets, breathing
   Of something beyond renown.

I walked with a proud defiance
   Of things that I could not see;
You leaned, with a sweet reliance,
   On One who was veiled to me.

But then came trouble and illness,
   And phantoms of doubt and fear;

And then the twilight and stillness,
    When Ethel, my friend, drew near.

I love her for all she brought me,
    The balm and the healing stream;
And now she has soothed and taught me,
    I, too, have begun to dream.

After the Tempest

There is silence in the forest,
    Now the storm is past;
After days of strife and wailing,
    Peace hath come at last.
Softly sings the quiet river
    'Neath a pallid sky,
And the grasses faintly quiver
    To the wind's low sigh.

There is silence in the forest
    As the day declines;
There are tears that fall at even
    O'er the smitten pines;
Low lies many a stately column,
    Stricken in its might,
And a voice comes, deep and solemn,
    Through the fading light:

"Some have but their branches shaken,
    Some are snapped in twain.
Who can tell why those were taken,
    Or why these remain?"
Through the silence of the forest
    Hear that warning call!
"Ye that deem ye stand securely,
    Take heed lest ye fall."

Children's Joys

The children's world is full of sweet surprises;
    Our common things are precious in their sight:
For them the stars shine, and the morning rises
    To show new treasures of untold delight;

A dance of blue-bells in the shady places;
    A crimson flush of sunset in the west;
The cobwebs, delicate as fairy laces;
    The sudden finding of a wood-bird's nest.

Their hearts and lips are full of simple praises
    To Him who made the earth divinely sweet;
They dwell among the buttercups and daisies,
    And find His blessings strewn about their feet.

But we, worn out by days of toil and sorrow,
    And sick of pleasures that are false and vain,
Would freely give our golden hoards to borrow
    One little hour of childhood's bliss again.

Yet He who sees their joy, beholds our sadness;
    And in the wisdom of a Father's love
He keeps the secret of the heavenly gladness:
    Our sweet surprises wait for us above.

By the Stream

Sweet tangled banks, where ox-eyed daisies grow
    And scarlet poppies gleam;
Sweet changing lights, that ever come and go
    Upon the quiet stream!

Once more I see the flash of splendid wings,
    As dragon-flies flit by;
Once more for me the small sedge-warbler sings
    Beneath a sapphire sky.

Once more I feel the simple, fresh content
    I found in stream and soil
When golden summers slowly came and went
    And mine was all their spoil.

I find amid the honeysuckle flowers
    And shy forget-me-not
Old boyish memories of lonely hours
    Passed in this silent spot.

Oh, God of Nature, how thy kindness keeps
    Some changeless things on earth!
And he who roams far off, and toils and weeps,
    Comes home to learn their worth.

Gay visions vanish, worldly schemes may fail,
    Hope prove an idle dream,
But still the blossoms flourish, red and pale,
    Beside my native stream.

Bygone Days

Weary, and full of sin,
    With fond desire,
I stand outside the church's open door,
And see the many-tinted lights that pour
Through jewelled windows on the marble floor
    From nave to choir.

I listen to the tide
    Of choral song;
A thousand voices through the arches ring,
Chanting the praises of the new-born King,
Glory to God, and peace on earth, they sing,
    Deep-toned and strong.

I think of bygone days
    When life was fair;
Ah me! if I could feel as once I felt
When meekly on that marble floor I knelt,
And found the girlish heart within me melt
    In fervent prayer!

Where is the steadfast faith
    That once was mine?
I followed learned lights and found them lead
From empty shrine to shrine, from creed to creed;
And then, O God, I knew, in bitter need,
    They were not Thine!

And now I come to Thee,
    Those wanderings past,
And listen to the simple Christmas strain,
Until I lose my load of doubt and pain,
And find my girlhood's faith and Christ again,
    The First and Last.

Going Down the Stream

Boughs that bend above the river
    Drop their blossom-showers,
And their bark goes drifting, drifting
    With the floating flowers;
How the little boat is gliding
    On, through gloom and gleam!
Softly moving, calmly sliding,
    Going down the stream.

Bees are humming, birds are singing,
    Swallows dart and glide;
But a warning voice comes ringing
    From the water-side.
"Stay, O friends, the tide is flowing
    Swifter than ye deem!"
"Life is sweet," they answer, going
    Smoothly down the stream.

Rich and warm the light is lying
    On the summer lands;
They, in full contentment sighing,
    Clasp each other's hands;
"Fools," the solemn voice cries, chiding,
    "Death will end the dream!"
"Life is bliss," they murmur, gliding
    Swiftly down the stream.

Whispers in the swaying rushes,
    Shadows o'er the skies;
On the rapid, darkling waters
    Beads of foam arise;
Startled eyes, to fear awaking,
    Seek the distant shore;
Through the spell of languor breaking
    Comes the torrent's roar!

Going Down the Stream

Speeds the small bark nearer, nearer
    To the foaming fall;
Hope and love and strength are wasted,
    Lost beyond recall;
All the wealth of God-sent gladness
    Bartered for a dream;
Thus they end their course of madness,
    Going down the stream.

An Ivy Song

In the mellow autumn sunshine,
    When the year was on the wane,
I dreamed a dream of earthly bliss
    That cannot come again.
The vesper lights were gleaming
    On a ruined castle tower,
And I stood there dreaming—dreaming,
    When the ivy was in flower.

Down below me lay the shadows
    Where the alder-bushes grew;
The fields were dim with golden mist,
    The sky was faintly blue;
No restless wind came creeping
    Through my still and leafy bower;
Life was sweet and pain was sleeping
    When the ivy was in flower.

Oh, the bonnie, burnished ivy
    Clings around the ruin yet!
My blissful dream is over now;
    I woke to vain regret.
But patience soothes repining,
    Sorrow brings a priceless dower,
And God's light will still be shining
    When the ivy is in flower.

River Voices

I wandered to the river-side
    One calm November day;
Brown rushes whispered to the tide,
    The sky was gold and grey,
And deep and slow through gloom and glow,
    The waters went their way.

"What were the rushes whispering,
    Like voices in a dream?"
"A quiet river-song we sing,
    A song of shade and gleam;
But thou hast known a sweeter tone
    Beside our gliding stream."

"What did the last leaves say to thee,
    Still clinging to the trees?"
"A little while, and we shall be
    Far blown across the leas;
But farther yet thy friend hath set
    His home beyond the seas."

"What murmured then the river-tide,
    Deep-voiced as solemn prayer?"
"Come quickly to my breast, and glide
    To one who needs thy care;
True love knows best where hearts may rest,
    And God is everywhere!"

Dreaming and Waking

I dreamt I was a child again, last night;
    Far through the land of sleep I wandering went
To the old paths of peace, and lost delight,
    And tarried in the valleys of content.

The dew was on my spirit, and the dust
    Of the world's highway clave not to my feet;
I breathed an atmosphere of love and trust,
    I gathered common flowers, and found them sweet.

I revelled in the sunshine, and was glad,
    I thought each sun-lit cloud an angel's wing;
Joy was my daily portion, to be sad
    Was but a sudden, dark imagining.

The dream was beautiful; but who would pay
    For such brief ecstasy, with grief like this?
How bitter is the waking of today,
    After the night's calm hours of childish bliss!

Yet is it well to murmur? There is One
    Who knows whereof our feeble frames are made;
He watched the child who sported in the sun,
    He sees the woman toiling in the shade.

The wound whose hidden bleeding makes me faint
    Under light burdens once sustained with ease;
The daily pain of patience and restraint;—
    Doth not my Lord take note of things like these?

Yea, as a father pitieth his own,
    So will He pity me;—through strife and tears
He leads me by a way I have not known
    To the dear rest of His "eternal years."

The old, sweet, childish faith may still be mine,
    Although my childhood's joys lie far away;—
A faith that simply clasps the Hand divine,
    And walks straight onward to the endless day.

My Sheep Hear My Voice

It is Thy voice that floats above the din,
    Clear as a silver bell;
We hear Thee, Saviour, through the strife of sin,
    Thy servants heed Thee well:
Beyond all others, through the upper air
    That voice comes pure and sweet,
Like chimes, that from a steeple tall and fair,
    Break o'er the clamorous street.

Not all, O Lord, may walk erect, and know
    The music of that sound;
Some-cannot hear Thee till their heads are low,
    Ay, level with the ground!
And yet, for them, heart-humbled and alone,
    Spurned as the crowds go by,
There is a power in the royal tone
    To set them up on high.

Thy sheep shall hear Thy, voice—on plain or hill,
    Through flood or wilderness,
In the green pastures, by the waters still,
    In joy, or sharp distress,
Thy call will reach them—sometimes loud and near,
    Then faint and far away;
O Thou good Shepherd, grant that heart and ear
    May listen, and obey!

The Fisher

Sorrow, and strife, and pain
Have crushed my spirit with relentless hand,
Long have I toiled, O Lord, and wrought in vain,
　　But still, at Thy command.

Into the wide blue sea,
Clinging to Thine own word, I cast the net;
Thy covenant, was made of old with me,
　　And I will trust Thee yet.

Lord, it is hard to stand
Waiting and watching in this silent toil,
While other fishers draw their nets to land,
　　And shout to see their spoil.

My strength fails unawares,
My hands are weak—my sight grows dim with tears;
My soul is burdened with unanswered prayers,
　　And sick of doubts and fears.

I see, across the deep,
The moon cast down her fetters, silver-bright,
As if to bind the ocean in his sleep
　　With links of living light.

I hear the roll and rush
Of waves that kiss the bosom of the beach;—
That soft sea-voice which ever seems to hush
　　The tones of human speech.

A breeze comes sweet and chill
Over the waters, and the night wanes fast;
His promise fails; the net is empty still,
　　And hope's old dreams are past!

Slow fade the moon and stars,
And in the east, the new dawn faintly shines

The Fisher

Through dim grey shadows, flecked with pearly bars,
    And level silver lines.

    But lo! what form is this
Standing beside me on the desolate shore?
I bow my knees; His garment's hem I kiss;
    Master, I doubt no more!

    "Draw in thy net, draw in,"
He cries, "behold the straining meshes break!"
Ah, Lord, the spoil I toiled so long to win
    Is granted for Thy sake!

    The rosy day blooms out
Like a full-blossomed flower; the joyous sea
Lifts up its voice; the winds of morning shout
    All glory, God, to Thee!

Donald Graeme

We quarreled, Donald Graeme and I,
    Yet how, I scarcely know;
A bitter word, a swift reply,
And then, a silence, and a sigh
    Before he turned to go.

I lingered in the autumn lane,
    Until the vesper light
That glittered on the cottage pane
Burnt low; and over sea and plain,
    Crept the chill breath of night.

A slow dawn struggled into life;
    Up rose a cruel wind,
It lashed the billows into strife;
It cut my creepers like a knife,
    And left no bloom behind.

All day from yonder angry sea
    The briny foam-clouds came;
The women hung about the quay,
And oh, the breaking heart in me
    That cried for Donald Graeme!

Ah, well for those who part and kiss
    Before the sun goes down!
Death leaves them a remembered bliss;
But what remains to those that miss
    Love's own immortal crown?

At last the gale was stilled and spent;
    When vesper lights were dim
The boat came in with sails all rent;
There are no words for that content
    Wherewith I welcomed him!

Donald Graeme

Lasses, the years that come and go
    Quench not one holy flame;
And while her locks are white as snow,
The old wife's heart is still aglow
    With love of Donald Graeme.

Her Dream

"Mother, they tell me a dream is true
Whenever it comes when dawn is new,
For then, I have heard the gossips say,
The mists of the brain are swept away,
And clear the eyes of the soul can see
The secret things that are yet to be;
I dreamed a dream while the dawn was new—
Oh, mother, what if my dream is true?

"I saw in my dream a murky sky,
And crested billows were leaping high,
Leaping and dashing in stormy play
On a shattered wreck, their helpless prey;
Rolling and breaking in clouds of foam
On my love's good ship that sailed from home;
The sea-gulls screamed, and the wild wind blew—
Oh, mother, what if the dream is true?"

Autumn went by like a story told,
And the girlish cheek grew pale and cold;
When last year's leaves were faded and shed,
A snowdrop rose from its garden bed;
The hoar-frost silvered the cottage pane,
When the flower of hope bloomed out again,
But skies were bright with a wintry blue;—
Could earth rejoice if that dream were true?

Days went and came, and the air was sweet
In fresh spring fields where the young lambs bleat;
When catkins covered the willow-trees,
Glad tidings came from the far-off seas
Of brave lives won from the hungry waves,
By Love that watches, and guards, and saves.
"Oh, mother," she said, "God only knew
My lad was safe, though the dream was true!"

Between the Lights

A little pause in life, while daylight lingers
  Between the sunset and the pale moonrise,
When daily labour slips from weary fingers,
  And soft grey shadows veil the aching eyes.

Old perfumes wander back from fields of clover
  Seen in the light of suns that long have set;
Beloved ones, whose earthly toil is over,
  Draw near, as if they lived among us yet.

Old voices call me, through the dusk returning,
  I hear the echoes of departed feet;—
And then I ask, with vain and troubled yearning,
  What is the charm that makes old things so sweet?

Must the old joys be evermore withholden?
  Even their memory keeps me pure and true;
And yet, from out Jerusalem the Golden
  God speaketh, saying, "I make all things new."

"Father," I cry, "the old must still be nearer;
  Stifle my love, or give me back the past!
Give me the fair old earth, whose paths are dearer
  Than all Thy shifting streets, and mansions vast."

Peace, peace,—the Lord of earth and heaven knoweth
  The human soul in all its heat and strife;—
Out of His throne no stream of Lethe floweth,
  But the clear river of eternal life.

He giveth life, ay, life in all its sweetness,
  Old loves, old sunny scenes will He restore;
Only the curse of sin and incompleteness
  Shall taint thine earth and vex thine heart no more.

Serve Him in daily work and earnest living,
  And faith shall lift thee to His sunlit heights;
Then shall a psalm of gladness and thanksgiving
  Fill the calm hour that comes between the lights.

Old Friends

Where are they scattered now,
  The old, old friends?
One made her dwelling where the maples glow,
And mighty streams through solemn forests flow,
Bat never, from that pine-crowned land of snow,
  A message sends.

Some meet me oft amid
  Life's common ways;
And then, perchance, a word or smile declares
That warm hearts throb beneath their load of cares;
For Love grows on, like wheat among the tares,
  Till harvest days.

"But some are fall'n asleep";[1]
  The words are sweet!
Oh, friends at rest beneath the blessed sod,
My feet still tread the weary road ye trod
Ere yet your loving souls went back to God!—
  When shall we meet?

Oh, Thou divinest Friend,
  When shall it be
That I may know them in their garments white?
And see them with a new and clearer sight,
Mine old familiar friends—made fair and bright,
  Like unto Thee!

1 1 Corinthians 15:6.

Deserted

Bright sea, far-flooding all the pebbled sand,
   Flinging thy foamy pearls from stone to stone;
Thy lullaby, low-murmured to the strand,
      Sounds like a lover's tone;
         And yet I know, elsewhere,
        Some other shore, as fair,
Thy waves have kissed, and left it dry and lone.

Bright sunshine, gleaming on my cottage wall,
   Tracing the shadow of an ivy-spray,
How tenderly thy golden touches fall
      On common things today!
        Yet, beneath other skies
        Some land benighted lies,
Deserted by thy glory, cold and grey.

Blithe bird, loud-warbling underneath the eaves
   An eager love-song passionate and shrill,
My heart is trembling amid summer leaves
      With sweet responsive thrill;
        Yet far away, dear guest,
        There Is an empty nest
Which thou hast left forsaken, void and still.

Fair sea, bright sunshine, bird of song divine,
   I too may lose the tide, the light, the lay;
Others may win the kisses that were mine,
      My night may be their day;
        Yet though the soul may sigh
        For precious things gone by,
I shall have had my rapture, come what may!

A Time of Peace

Golden leaves, and a golden day;
  (Lights are warm when the year is old:)
Rushes whisper, and branches sway,
Gossamer shines and drifts away,
And the empty fort is still and grey;
  (The river flows like a tide of gold.)

Long ago from that dim hill-crest
  (The year was young, and lights were pale:)
Brake the thunder that scared the rest
Out of the rich vale's languid breast,
Till day died faint in the clouded west;
  (But only the river tells the tale.)

Golden rays are about your face,
  (Mellow lights are the old year's crown;)
Come to the old war-haunted place;
Come with your spell of peace and grace
To the heart where strife has scared its trace;
  (The river sings as the sun goes down.)

Golden ways are before our feet;
  (While the year wanes the rich light glows:)
Life is stored with the garnered wheat,
All the bitter has turned to sweet,
After the battle the rest is meet;
  (The song goes on as the river flows.)

At Rest

Ah, silent wheel, the noisy brook is dry.
    And quiet hours glide by
In this deep vale, where once the merry stream
    Sang on through gloom and gleam;
Only the dove in some leaf-shaded nest
    Murmurs of rest.

Ah, weary voyager, the closing day
    Shines on that tranquil bay,
Where thy storm-beaten soul has longed to be;
    Wild blast and angry sea
Touch not this favoured shore, by summer blest,
    A home of rest.

Ah, fevered heart, the grass is green and deep
    Where thou art laid asleep;
Kissed by soft winds, and washed by gentle showers,
    Thou hast thy crown of flowers,
Poor heart, too long in this mad world opprest,
    Take now thy rest.

I too, perplex'd with strife of good and ill,
    Long to be safe and still;
Evil is present with me while I pray
    That good may win the day;
Great Giver, grant me Thy last gift and best,
    The gift of rest!

Arlette

A Man's Remembrance

The day is spent, and fields, new-shorn,
    Are bright with fading sheen;
Like blossoms left behind the corn,
    The maidens come and glean;
Blue eyes, and floating locks of gold,
    Have caught you in their net;
You smile, and call me strange and cold—
    You never knew Arlette.

I met her when this life of mine
    Had turned from sweet to sour:
There was no sparkle in the wine,
    No bloom upon the flower.
I roamed away to bear alone
    The stings of vain regret;
The grain was gone, the reapers flown,
    When first I found Arlette.

The glamour of the "sunny south"
    About her beauty lies;
A mellow cheek, a scarlet mouth,
    And dark, beseeching eyes;
A daughter of the soil, as sweet
    As summer buds dew-wet;
No taint of our town-bred deceit
    Has ever touched Arlette.

With half her charm some girls might win
    A fashionable fame;
How came she with that southern skin,
    And soft old Norman name?
We talked, I questioned, she replied,
    Till I forgot my fret;
For bitter thoughts and angry pride
    All fled before Arlette.

Arlette

How ends the tale? To your surprise
    There is no end to tell!
I left no tears in those dark eyes,
    Although I loved them well;
Her picture hangs within my brain
    Fresh and unsullied yet;
No empty vows of mine shall pain
    The heart of true Arlette.

But, when my harvest-field appears
    As bare as it can be,
She comes, and finds some golden ears
    Of life's good grain for me;
My old belief in truth and trust
    She brings back, sometimes yet;
You smile again;—ah, well, you must;
    You never knew Arlette.

My Nell

A Soliloquy—Founded on Beranger

You are nobly-born, I know,
    Rich, and beautiful, and free;
And they tell me (is it so?)
    That you waste a thought on me!
In your hazel eyes last night
    There was tenderness and truth;
But there came a softer light
    To the poet in his youth.
I can give you high esteem,
    Gracious friend, and lovely belle;
But I cannot love you now
    As I used to love my Nell.

We were paupers, she and I,
    And the bread was hard to win;
But our garret near the sky
    Let God's purest sunlight in.
She was meanly dressed, you see,
    In her faded cotton gown;
But her smile was heaven to me,
    And I never saw her frown.
You are like a rose in June,
    She was but a lily-bell;
Yet I cannot love you now
    As I used to love my Nell.

We were young, and life was sweet,
    And we loved each other more
When there scarce was food to eat,
    And the wolf was at the door.
There was always hope, you know;
    We could dream that skies were blue;
But—my darling had to go
    Just before the dream came true!

My Nell

I am left alone with fame,
   And the great world likes me well;
But I cannot love again
   As I used to love my Nell.

Then forgive me if the light
   Of your presence leaves me cold;
You are young, and gay, and bright,
   I am growing grave and old;
And the brow *she* used to kiss
   Is more wrinkled than of yore,
But the treasure that I miss
   Is not lost, but gone before.
Some have many loves, but I
   Learnt to love but once, and well;
And I cannot woo you now
   As I used to woo my Nell.

Relics

A spray of oak-leaves and some withered flowers,
    Gathered by hands that loved to cling to mine;
Poor relics of the joys that once were ours,
      The days of shade and shine!

I touch the leaves, and hear your voice again,
    Telling the old sweet story o'er and o'er,
Till I forget the doubt—the change—the pain—
      The sorrow strange and sore.

The past revives, I dream our early dream
    Of Alpine blossoms on a fragrant sod,
Of far, white glories, where the snow-peaks gleam,
      And lift our souls to God.

Of some lone châlet by a deep blue lake,
    Where life is full of simple, calm delights,
And we might watch the rosy morning break
      Across the solemn heights.

The visions fade;—the hopes that gave them rise
    Have perished, and the love has had its day;
My path lies lonely beneath English skies,
      And yours is far away.

Yet I press onward, though the way be dim,
    And thorns spring up where roses used to blow;
Through dawn and darkness I will follow Him
      Who called me long ago.

He bade me leave the things I love the best;
    I held them back from His entreating hand;
He offered peace; I chose my own unrest,
      And would not understand.

And still His patience never knew decay,
    And still He waited for the certain end;

Relics

There came a storm that swept my joys away,
  And then I knew my Friend.

I knew Him by the crown of cruel thorn
  That sinful hands had woven for His head,
And by His promise—"Blest are they that mourn;
  They shall be comforted."

And finding One in whom my soul can trust,
  I turn my face from dreams that proved untrue,
Leaving old relics crumbling in the dust;
  For Christ makes all things new.

Therefore your voice has lost the charm of old,
  You cannot bind me with a broken spell;
The song is ended, and the tale is told,
  And thus I say—farewell.

The Slow Stream

Ah me! I said, the stream is slow,
  My spirit chides delay;
How languidly its waters flow
  Throughout the summer day!
It creeps along with sleepy song,
  And loiters on the way.

Beneath the ivied arch it seems
  To pause in dusky rest,
As if it wearied of the beams
  Of sunlight on its breast,
And loved to sleep in shadows deep,
  By willow-boughs caressed.

It dallies with the golden flowers
  In meadows cool and green,
And murmurs under feudal towers
  Of glories that have been;
Too long it stays in woodland ways
  Among the ferns, I ween.

There waits an eager heart for me
  Far on the shining main;
It is the sea, the open sea,
  My soul is sick to gain.
To moss and stone in dreamy tone
  The river mocks my pain.

"Oh, peace," my guardian angel sighed
  (His voice was sweet and low),
"Love, work, and pray, and day by day
  The stream will faster flow;
It rests with thee, if Time shall be
  A river swift or slow."

My Little Woman

A homely cottage, quaint and old,
Its thatch grown thick with green and gold,
    And wind-sown grasses;
Unchanged it stands in sun and rain,
And seldom through the quiet lane
    A footstep passes.

Yet here my little woman dwelt,
And saw the shroud of winter melt
    From meads and fallows;
And heard the yellow-hammer sing
A tiny welcome to the spring
    From budding sallows.

She saw the early morning sky
Blush with a tender wild-rose dye
    Above the larches;
And watched the crimson sunset burn
Behind the summer plumes of fern
    In woodland arches.

My little woman, gone away
To that far land which knows, they say,
    No more sun-setting!
I wonder if her gentle soul,
Securely resting at the goal,
    Has learnt forgetting?

My heart wakes up, and cries in vain;
She gave me love, I gave her pain
    While she was living;
I knew not when her spirit fled,
But those who stood beside her, said
    She died forgiving.

My dove has found a better rest,
And yet I love the empty nest

She left neglected;
I tread the very path she trod,
And ask—in her new home with God
    Am I expected?

If it were but the Father's will
To let me know she loves me still,
    This aching sorrow
Would turn to hope, and I could say,
Perchance she whispers day by day,
    "He comes tomorrow."

I linger in the silent lane,
And high above the clover plain
    The clouds are riven;
Across the fields she used to know
The light breaks, and the wind sighs low,
    "Loved and forgiven."

Under the Apple-Tree

A dome of blossom rises overhead,
    Piled like the snows upon some Alpine height,
And blushing with such tints of pink and red
    As summer clouds may wear in vesper light.

Dew-spangled—pierced with sudden shafts of gold
    That slide between the latticed boughs below;
A little world of bloom, that seems to fold
    Birds, bees, and sunbeams in a tender glow.

Life is so sweet beneath this fairy bower
    That the full heart must tremble in its bliss,
And fear lest wanton breeze or hasty shower
    Should harm one petal by a careless kiss.

Under the apple-tree I stand alone,
    In the strange stillness of an autumn day:
Where have the swallows and the brown bees flown?
    What cruel hand hath snatched my blooms away?

The sullen, silver-rifted sky looks down
    Between grey branches,—not a golden gleam
Falls on the scanty leaves, grown sere and brown;
    And I am haunted by that flowery dream!

O foolish heart!—beside the mossy root
    Lie the rich spoils that put thy grief to shame!
He takes the blossom, but He gives the fruit,
    That men may magnify His worthy name.

He gives a treasure for a vanished toy,
    Filling the soul before its void is known;
A solid blessing for a fragile joy
    His hand bestows:—make thou His gifts thine own.

At Richmond

The sun-god's parting shafts of gold
  Quivered and fell on field and wood;
And silent, as in hours of old,
  Upon the river-bank we stood;
Did not that waning glory cast
  A charm upon the flowing tide,
And give us back the summers past—
  The bloom that fled—the lights that died?

Silent, and filled with strange delight,
  We watched the sunset brightness fade;
And felt the first cool breath of night
  Creep up through mist and mellow shade;
It whispered of a time of rest,
  Of pain outlived, and labour done,
When all the things we count the best
  And live for, shall be fairly won.

And even in life's rugged ways
  These happy thoughts of peace return,
For we have learnt to fix our gaze
  Beyond the bounds which men discern;
We know not where God's river flows,
  Nor when its waves shall wash our feet,
And yet, each foretaste of repose
  He gives us is divinely sweet.

After a Night of Weeping

When the long night of weariness and pain
   Is full of bitter thoughts, and doubts that sting,
Do we not long to hear some holy strain
      That far-off angels sing?

When every golden deed the heart hath planned
   Is darkened by the fear of failing powers,
And all our life seems like a barren land,
      Unbless'd by sun and showers.

When every word that loving lips have said
   Sounds, to the morbid fancy, falsely sweet;
And every truth that we have heard or read
      Seems poor and incomplete.

When the one thing whereon our hopes are set
   Is still withheld, although we pray and weep,
Until we murmur "Can the Lord forget?
      Or doth the Master sleep?"

When the old sin that we had nearly crushed,
   Arrayed in all its fearful might appears,
And yearning voices that we thought were hushed,
      Call from departed years.

Then, like an evening wind that unperceived
   Beareth an odor from the rose's breast,
Comes the remembrance: "We which have believed
      Do enter into rest."

And our eyes close, and all the phantom throng
   Of doubts and troubles vanish into air;
And the one face that we have loved so long,
      Smiles on us calm and fair.

The face that in our darkest hour is bright,
   The tranquil brow that never wears a frown,

After a Night of Weeping

The steadfast eyes, that never lose their light
    Beneath the thorny crown.

So at his word the clouds are all withdrawn,
    The small, sharp pains of life are soothed away;
After the night of weeping comes the dawn,
    And then, his perfect day.

London Twilight

The winter day is fading fast,
　A day of bitter wind and sleet;
And dreaming of a brighter past
　I sit and gaze across the street.

A little girl with sunny hair
　Stands looking through the window-pane,
And sees a future May-time fair,
　With clearer skies and softer rain.

My heart goes backward, miles and miles,
　To gather withered leaves and flowers,
But on her hopeful fancy smiles
　The bright new green of summer bowers.

Her trusting glances, never dim,
　Pierce swiftly through the twilight haze,
And meet the tender face of Him
　Whose love is watching both our ways.

Ah, little girl, across the street
　My spirit flies to learn of thine!
Thy childish faith, so calm and sweet,
　Is wiser than all thoughts of mine.

For hope is better than regret,
　And one who loves us both may be
Waiting beside still waters yet
　In pastures green to welcome me.

Two Seasons

Can this be spring? These tearful lights that break
    Across wet uplands in the windy dawn
Are paler than the primroses, that make
    Dim glories on the banks of field and lawn;
Wild blasts are sweeping o'er the garden beds,
    Wild clouds are drifting through the dull, grey skies,
And early flowers, rain-beaten, hang their heads;
    Can it be spring that wears this stormy guise?

Can this be autumn? Freshly green and fair
    The meadows glisten in the morning rays,
Touches of brown and crimson, here and there,
    Are all that tell us that the year decays.
We would not have the old year young again;
    If this be death, we find him passing sweet;
Watching the soft hues change on hill and plain,
    We wait in peace the calm destroyer's feet.

A Song of Land at Sea

"Now would I give a thousand furlongs of sea for an acre of barren ground; long heath, brown furze, anything."—TEMPEST, SCENE I.

Soft wind, low piping through the shrouds all day,
Dost thou not whisper of the woods to me?
Oh for thy wings, that I might speed away
Over this trackless waste of weary sea!

Sing on, sweet wind, a song of summer leaves,
Lisping, through trembling shadows in the lane,
Of roses nodding under moss-grown eaves,
Of raindrops tinkling on the cottage pane.

Under thy pinions bent the springing wheat,
The large field-daisies bowed their starry crowns,
The wild thyme sighed to thee, and faintly sweet
The scent of gorse was blown across the downs.

Soft wind, low piping through the shrouds to me,
What would I give to roam where thou hast been!
A thousand furlongs of this restless sea
For one lone mile of moor or woodland green!

A Buried Love

Our love was born amid the purple heather,
  When winds were still, and vesper lights were red;
For one bright year we cherished it together;
    Now, it lies cold and dead.

Dead; and across the brown hill-ridges, wailing,
  Comes the wild autumn in her swift return,
With sullen tears, and misty garments trailing
    Over the faded fern.

Ah, there may come a time—God send it quickly—
  When love's lone grave shall wear a fragrant wreath
Of blooms, and velvet mosses, piling thickly
    Upon the dust beneath.

And we, across the heather slow returning,
  May seek, perchance, this sacred mound of ours;
Seek it, unvexed by any foolish yearning,
    And find it lost in flowers.

May Memories

Swiftly wound the silver river
  Where the grass grew deep,
Through the mystic shade and silence
  That the woodlands keep;
Underneath the chestnuts straying,
  (Trembling fans o'erhead,)
With the creamy blossoms playing,
  How my bright hours sped!

As a dream when one awaketh
  Seems to me that day,
Chestnut blossoms, sliding river,
  Fairyland of May!
City walls close in behind me,
  Summer joys are o'er;
Where the sunshine used to find me
  I shall stray no more.

Other hands will pull the blossoms,
  Cones of pink and white;
Mine are worn with daily labor,
  Tired from morn till night;
Still I muse, but not in sadness,
  On those bygone days;
Here my autumn hath its gladness
  Worth a thousand Mays!

Old Home

"Return, return," the voices cried,
  "To your old valley, far away;
For softly on the river tide
  The tender lights and shadows play;
And all the banks are gay with flowers,
  And all the hills are sweet with thyme;
Ye cannot find such bloom as ours
    In yon bright foreign clime!"

And still "Return, return," they sung,
  "With us abides eternal calm;
In these old fields, where you were young,
  We cull the heart's-ease and the balm;
For us the flocks and herds increase,
  And children play around our feet;
At eve the sun goes down in peace—
    Return, for rest is sweet."

For me, I thought, the olives grow,
  The sun lies warm upon the vines;
And yet, I will arise and go
  To that dear valley dim with pines.
Old loves are dwelling there, I said,
  Untouched by years of change and pain;
Old faiths, that I had counted dead,
    Shall rise, and live again.

Then I arose, and crossed the sea,
  And sought that home of younger days;
No love of old was left to me
  (For Love has wings, and seldom stays);
But there were graves upon the hill,
  And sunbeams shining on the sod,
And low winds breathing, "Peace, be still;
    Lost things are found in God."

A Rising Tide

The west wind clears the morning,
   The sea shines silver-grey;
The night was long, but fresh and strong
   Awakes the breezy day;
Like smoke that flies across the lift,
   The clouds are faint and thin;
And near and far, along the bar,
   The tide comes creeping in.

The dreams of midnight showed me
   A life of loneliness,
A stony shore, that knew no more
   The bright wave's soft caress;
The morning broke, the visions fled,—
   With dawn new hopes begin;
The light is sweet, and at my feet
   The tide comes rolling in.

Over the bare, black boulders
   The ocean sweeps and swells;
Oh, waters wide, ye come to hide
   Dull stones and empty shells!
I hear the floods lift up their voice
   With loud, triumphant din;
Sad dreams depart,—rest, doubting heart,
   The tide comes foaming in!

Room for the Wanderer

Room for the wanderer, room!
    The gates stand open wide;
Hasten ere falls the midnight gloom.
    To Jesus crucified.

Room in the crimson tide
    Of Christ's most precious blood;
Safe shelter in His wounded side,
    Whence flow'd the healing flood!

Room in that city bright,
    That city up above,
Where saints, in robes of purest white
    Forever sing His love!

God's message rings sublime,
    Its voice let all obey:
Lo, this is the accepted time;
    Lo, this is Mercy's day!

Saviour, As This Hour Is Ending

Saviour, as this hour is ending,
 Once again on Thee we call.
Let Thy Holy Dove, descending,
 Bring Thy mercy to us all;
Set thy seal on every heart;
 Jesus, bless us ere we part!

Bless the gospel message, spoken
 In Thine own appointed way;
Give each longing soul a token
 Of Thy tender love today;
Set thy seal on every heart;
 Jesus, bless us ere we part!

Comfort those in pain or sorrow;
 Watch each anxious child of Thine;
Grant us hope for each tomorrow,
 Strengthened by Thy grace divine;
Set thy seal on every heart;
 Jesus, bless us ere we part!

Pardon Thou each deed unholy;
 Lord, forgive each sinful thought;
Make us contrite, pure, and lowly,
 By Thy great example taught;
Set thy seal on every heart;
 Jesus, bless us ere we part!

Saviour Thou Knowest the Souls that Are Dreary

Saviour, thou knowest the souls that are dreary,
    Songless and sad as these desolate stones;
Hearts that would welcome thee yet are too weary,
    Voices that give thee but sorrowful tones;
Thou art the bringer of hope to the cheerless,
    Thou art the giver of peace after strife;
Teach them to cling to thee, trusting and fearless,
    Lord of their life, Lord of their life!

Come, as the healer of hearts that are broken,
    Come when our sunshine is wintry and pale;
Hearer of pleadings that never were spoken,
    Thou art the same, and thy love cannot fail;
Enter the chamber that light has forsaken,
    Bring back the gladness of happier days,
Come, and the joy of thy presence shall waken
    Songs to thy praise, Songs to thy praise.

How Long?

At evening time it shall be light.—Zechariah 14:7.

The weary hours like shadows come and go,
　　As still I strive, by earnest faith and prayer:
To do each day the duties that I know,
　　And bear the Cross my Saviour bids me bear.

But are there many weary miles to tread
　　Before the promised home appears in sight?
And are there sad and bitter tears to shed
　　Ere we shall meet in realms of endless light?

Some little joy I have in doing still
　　The humble work He bids me do for Him;
A tender gladness when 'tis mine to fill
　　Again some empty chalice to the brim.

And thus the days are slowly passing here,
　　With distant gleams of hope and glory blest;
But is the hallowed moment drawing near
　　When we shall meet again in endless rest?

Ah, yes, when that great light which men call Death
　　Strikes thro' the gloom and stills at last the strife,
Then comes a hush, a sigh, a fleeting breath,
　　And we shall meet again in endless life.

We Sing a Loving Jesus

We sing a loving Jesus
    Who left His throne above,
And came on earth to ransom
    The children of His love;
It is an oft told story
    And yet we love to tell
How Christ, the King of glory,
    Once deigned with man to dwell.

We sing a holy Jesus;
    No taint of sin defiled
The Babe of David's city,
    The pure and stainless child:
O teach us, blessed Saviour,
    Thy heavenly grace to seek,
And let our whole behaviour,
    Like Thine, be mild and meek.

We sing a lowly Jesus,
    No Kingly crown He had:
His heart was bowed with anguish,
    His face was marred and sad;
In deep humiliation
    He came, His work to do;
O Lord of our salvation,
    Let us be humble too.

We sing a mighty Jesus,
    Whose voice could raise the dead;
The sightless eyes He opened,
    The famished souls He fed.
Thou earnest to deliver
    Mankind from sin and shame;
Redeemer and life giver,
    We praise Thy holy Name!

We Sing a Loving Jesus

We sing a coming Jesus;
    The time is drawing near,
When Christ with all His Angels
    In glory shall appear;
Lord, save us, we entreat Thee,
    In this Thy day of grace,
That we may gladly meet Thee,
    And see Thee face to face.

The Master Is Come

The Master is come, and calleth for thee.—JOHN 11:28.

The Master hath come, and He calls us to follow,
    The track of the footprints He leaves on our way;
Far over the mountain, and through the deep hollow,
    The path leads us on to the mansions of day.

The Master hath called us, the children who fear Him,
    Who march 'neath Christ's banner, His own little band;
We love Him, and seek Him; we long to be near Him,
    And rest in the light of His beautiful land.

The Master hath called us; the road may be dreary,
    And dangers and sorrows are strewn on the track;
But God's Holy Spirit shall comfort the weary,—
    We follow the Saviour, and cannot turn back.

The Master hath called us; though doubt and temptation
    May compass our journey, we cheerfully sing,
"Press onward, look upward"; through much tribulation
    The children of Sion must follow their King!

The Master hath called us; in life's early morning,
    With spirits as fresh as the dew on the sod;
We turn from the world, with its smiles and its scorning,
    To cast in our lot with the people of God.

The Master hath called us His sons and His daughters,
    We plead for His blessing, and trust in His love;
And through the green pastures, beside the still waters,
    He'll lead us at last to His kingdom above.

We Praise Our Lord Today

Lead me and guide me.—PSALM 31:3.

We praise our Lord today
For love and light and peace;
He leads us in the narrow way,
His care can never cease.

He guides our failing feet,
Each fainting heart He cheers;
He shields us in the noontide heat,
And calms our midnight fears.

When lone and sad and worn,
His presence makes us blest;
For Jesus comforts those that mourn,
And gives the weary rest.

The angel hosts above,
His holy Name adore,
And we the children of His love
Should praise Him evermore.

We long to see His face,
To know as we are known,
And wear the spotless robes of grace
Before the great white throne.

Now the Solemn Shadows Darken

Hearken unto the supplications of Thy servant, and of Thy People, and when Thou hearest, forgive.—1 KINGS 8:30.

Now the solemn shadows darken,
    And the daylight slowly dies;
Holy Saviour, Thou wilt hearken
    When Thy children's prayers arise:
      Blessèd Jesus,
    Look on us with loving eyes.

Some are tried with doubts and dangers,
    Some have found their hearts grow cold,
Some are aliens now and strangers
    To the faith they loved of old:
      Blessèd Jesus,
    Bring them back into the fold.

Some in conflict sore have striven
    With temptation fierce and strong;
Lord, to them let strength be given,
    If the battle should be long;
      Blessed Jesus,
    Change their mourning into song.

By Thy passion in the garden,
    By Thine anguish on the tree,
By that precious gift of pardon,
    Won for us alone by Thee,
      Blessèd Jesus,
    Set the sin-bound captives free.

When our earthly day is closing,
    And the night grows still and deep,
Let us, in Thine arms reposing,
    Feel Thy power to save and keep;
      Blessèd Jesus,
    Give Thine own beloved, sleep.

Ready to Depart

Her step grows slower on the flowery sward;
Friend after friend draws nigh with aching heart,
And whispers, "Lo, the handmaid of the Lord
    Is ready to depart."

They ask her if she weeps for summers flown,
For the old hopes—the old loves tried and true?
She answers, "He that sitteth on the throne
    Saith 'I make all things new.'"

They ask her if she feels no vain regret,
For joys that stand like earth's ungathered grain?
She answers, "Christ hath richer harvests yet;
    For me, to die is gain."

They ask her if she has no tear to shed,
For her old home amid the pleasant lands?
She answers, "God shall give me in its stead
    A house not made with hands."

Thus calmly trusting in the Saviour's grace
She rests upon the margin of the tide,
And sees the light of her fair dwelling-place
    Upon the other side.

Beyond It All

I hear a gladsome wind that sings
    In budding copse and waving grass;
And on the hill, like living things,
    The light cloud-shadows slowly pass;
How soon from forests far away
    Will ring the wood-dove's summer call,
And roses open day by day!
    But I shall go beyond it all.

Beyond the hopes of life and time;
    The songs that end when sunshine dies;
The blooms that wither in their prime;
    The passing blush of evening skies;
Beyond the chill of rains that beat
    On flowers that fade, and leaves that fall;
Beyond the bitter and the sweet;—
    Beyond it all, beyond it all!

Beyond the fitful light and shade;
    The idols crumbling into dust;
The graves where patient hearts have laid
    Their memories of love and trust;
The voices that have changed their tone;
    The dreams that fly; the joys that pall;
The griefs that only One has known;—
    Beyond them all, beyond them all!

I thank Thee, Father, for the thought
    That all the work of life is done;
The story told, the battle fought,
    The rest eternal nearly won.
Thy love has kept me till the end,
    My waiting spirit hears Thee call;
Draw near, O never-changing Friend,
    And guide me home—beyond it all!

Hidden Life

I stood by her quiet grave in May,
The dancing shadows of leaf and spray,
And drooping boughs of laburnum gold
Swept softly over the turf and mould;
The lilac-blossoms came down in showers,
And the chestnuts shed their milk-white flowers;
My tears fell fast on the fragrant sod—
But her life was hid with Christ in God.

I stood by the peaceful grave again,
When the grass was wet with autumn rain;
A rose, that summer had left behind,
Swung to and fro in the wailing wind;
While leaf after leaf came fluttering down,
Amber, and crimson, and tawny brown;
My tears fell fast on the moss-grown sod—
But her life was hid with Christ in God.

I stood by her grave in early spring,
The first white snowdrop, a slender thing,
Came peeping out of the chilly mould;
I thought of the Saviour's words of old,
While over our silent dead we weep
He comes "to awake them out of sleep!"
I gave Him thanks by the quiet sod—
That her life was hid with Christ in God.

Evening Hymn at Sea

Then they that were in the ship came and worshipped Him.
*—*Matthew 14:33.

We come to Thee, sweet Saviour, humbly seeking
    Thy shelter when the darkness draweth nigh;
Fain would our listening spirits hear Thee speaking;
    Be with us, Lord, and whisper, "It is I."

Comfort Thy weary ones, whose hearts are bending
    Beneath the burdens of this world of care;
Show them in dreams "the life that hath no ending,"
    And tell them of the joy that waits them there.

Hold all our dear ones safely in Thy keeping,
    Give them bright thoughts of Thee and tranquil rest;
Shine on the far-off homes where they are sleeping,
    Bless them, sweet Saviour, and they shall be blest!

If there be tears on some beloved faces,
    Smile on them, Jesus, chase their grief away;
O bid Thine angels fill our vacant places,
    Watching the friends we love by night and day.

A word of Thine can still the troubled ocean,
    Thy Spirit moves upon the pathless deep;
We lift our prayers to Thee in meek devotion,
    And, guarded by Thy mercy, softly sleep.

Oh! by Thy Name upon our hearts engraven,
    And by the blood that bought our souls for Thee,
Bring us at last unto that blessed haven
    Where there is no more night and no more sea!
                           Amen.

Watching

When the Son of Man cometh, shall He find faith on the earth?
—LUKE 18:8.

When Thy virgins' lamps are burning,
  While the slow hours creep,
Wilt Thou suddenly returning
  Break their weary sleep?

When the busy hands are idle
  And the strong hearts fail,
Will the summons to the Bridal
  Rend the cloudy veil?

When the crimson morning faintly
  O'er the East shall break,
Will there be no spirits saintly
  Watching for Thy sake?

Will there be no faithful servant
  Looking for Thy sign?
Prayerful, hopeful, strong and fervent,
  Fill'd with love divine;

Love, that ever more remembers
  All the old desires,
Fanning still the glowing embers
  Of its beacon fires!

Yea, upon the wind-swept heather
  Of the cloudy hill,
Christian souls keep watch together,
  Waiting for Thee still.

Yea, within the valleys lowly,
  On the quiet sod,
Christian hearts keep vigil holy
  For the Son of God.

Watching

In the great world's crowded places
    Some whose hopes are high,
Listen with uplifted faces
    For the Herald's cry:

Trusting, pleading, weeping, fearing,
    Scorning earthly things;
Through the wild sin-revel hearing
    Sounds of angel-wings.

Sorrowful, yet fill'd with gladness,
    Bound,—yet always free;
Strangers in a land of sadness,—
    Yet well known to Thee.

Poor,—yet often richly giving
    From their secret hoard;
Dying daily,—and yet living
    Ever to the Lord.

These are Thine;—O Bridegroom, hear them
    When their cries ascend!
Let Thy Comforter be near them
    Till their watch shall end.

Guard them,—till Thine angel loudly
    Sounds the trumpet blast,
And Thou comest, crownèd proudly,
    As a King, at last!

In Memory of Bishop Patteson

Hath He who reaps the wheat and leaves the tares,
Who saves the rotten tree and fells the sound,
No hidden purpose in the will that spares
　　The cumberers of the ground?

Thousands will live their lives, unloved, unblest;
Long selfish lives of sinful sloth and ease,
While he—the Martyr Bishop—lies at rest
　　In the far Southern Seas.

Better like him to spend a busy day,
Than pass whole years in idle waste and wrong,
For truly saith the poet in his lay
　　That "no true life is long."

Better to die for love of God and man,
Than live for lower aims and baser deeds,
Better to die "in faith"—than live to scan
　　Flaws in our neighbours' creeds.

He needs no praise of human lip or pen,
Nor "storied window" in the minster high,
His name is graven in the hearts of men,
　　His works will never die.

Soon shall the precious seed his hands have sown,
A goodly growth of golden blessings yield;
A fairer monument than carven stone
　　Is that rich harvest field.

So let us leave him—is it not in vain
On God's decrees to spend our idle breath?
Enough for us to live—and humbly gain
　　Strength from the Martyr's death.

Nothing but Leaves

Saviour, comest Thou to me
Seeking fruit upon Thy tree?
Shall I render naught to Thee?

Lively faith and holy deeds
Springing from His precious seeds,
Are the fruit the Searcher needs.

Shall His love and tender care,
Gifts of light and dew and air,
Win no guerdon for Him there?

Oft the Holy Spirit grieves
O'er the promise that deceives,
Seeking fruit, He finds but leaves:

Fair pretence and pleasant show
Hiding barrenness below,
Vain profession, working woe.

Only leaves;—O patient Lord,
After all Thy tears outpour'd
Shalt Thou find such poor reward?

After all Thy toil and pain,
Some return for love to gain,
Master, shalt Thou seek in vain?

Lest I prove a worthless tree,
Send Thy plenteous grace to me;
Let me bring forth fruit to Thee.

The Felled Tree

Trembling shadows, scatter'd gleams of glory,
    Where the summer sunlight falls and breaks
Over wrinkled roots and branches hoary,
    Dropping here and there in golden flakes.

Diamond dews upon the hawthorns twinkle,
    Merle and mavis pipe their mellow lay;
And like fairy chimes the sheep-bells tinkle
    Faintly from the pastures far away.

Low it lies—the stately forest giant,
    Stretch'd upon the ferns and grasses sweet;
All the winter long it stood defiant
    Of the bitter blast and driving sleet.

All the winter long it bore the burden
    Of the frozen snowflakes chill and white;
Waiting calmly for the summer's guerdon,
    Dancing leaves, soft wind, and golden light.

Wild March breezes sang and whistled loudly,
    April smiled and wept her silver tears,
Bright May blossom'd,—and the tree stood proudly,
    Robed in "living green," among its peers.

June's blue heaven shone upon her roses,
    Larks trill'd high above the growing corn;
One sweet day in song and perfume closes,
    And the tree lies low at early morn.

Smitten by the axe, and cleft asunder
    In the gladness of a summer hour;
Did it bear the storm and brave the thunder,
    Thus to perish in its day of power?

Better thus to die than live forgotten;
    Better fall while trunk and limbs are sound,

Than endure for ages sear'd and rotten,
　　As a cumberer of God's fair ground.

Not in pity of thy fallen beauty
　　Should we mourn for thee, O forest friend!
May our lives like thine be strong in duty,
　　May we make, like thee, a noble end.

Matins

Within the holy walls,
How calm it is! The mellow chastened light
Soothes the tired heart, and on the aching sight
    In benediction falls.

    The solemn deep-voiced bells!
Alas! some hearts refuse to hear their chime,
Nor heed the message, tender, yet sublime,
    Each lingering cadence tells.

    They ring out loud and clear,
The sonorous bells from yonder steeple tall;
And the pure morning sunshine loves to fall
    On God's fair temple here.

    Such will not brook delay;
But seek at once the great world and its care,
And from their round of toil are loth to spare
    The first hours of the day.

    How eagerly they pour
Into the busy mart and crowded street;
How quickly do they turn their weary feet
    Far from the church's door!

    Blind souls! They cannot know,
How at this very door the Saviour stands,
And stretches out to them those bleeding hands,
    Pierced for them long ago.

    Oh, that their eyes could see
The sweet sad Face they pass unheeding by,
While God-like pathos echoes in His cry,
    "Ye will not come to Me!"

    The tinted rays have kissed
The altar's marble steps, where woven lie

Topaz and sapphire, and rich emerald dye,
    Blending with amethyst.

        Like summer's balmy showers,
The sweet familiar words of these old prayers
Fill the soul's empty chalice unawares,
        In the still morning hours.

        We need a precious store
Of grace divine to last us through the day,
And keep our hearts from fainting on the way,
        When pressed and burdened sore.

The Sleep of Sorrow

Through the dim and quiet chamber, morning sunlight faintly shines,
Tracing quaint and chequered patterns, barred with slender golden lines
O'er the walls, and on the pillow where that weary head reclines.

All night long her bitter sorrow, slumber from her eyelids kept,
All night long her brow was aching, while she sighed, and prayed, and
    wept;
And the dawn rose grey and holy ere the troubled watcher slept.

Lo! a light wind rises singing from the very gates of day,
Gently stirs the feathered tree-tops, shaking showers of silver spray
From the leaves and scented blossoms o'er the mossy woodland way.

All the busy world is waking fresh and joyous from its rest;
Softly coos the happy ring-dove, brooding o'er her leafy nest,
And the brown bee hovers gaily o'er the cowslip's yellow crest.

Still she sleeps,—awhile forgetting all that heavy load of care,
Dreaming of a lightened burden, dreaming of an answered prayer.
Father, watch her when she wakens, give her strength the cross to bear.

Send some sweet and loving token to the heart so sorely tried,
Grant Thy gift of blessed patience, that her grief be sanctified;
Lead her swiftly, safely homeward, O Thou never-failing Guide.

Tell her that "a rest remaineth" for each worn and weary one;
Rest which comes with finished labour,—peace when this world's strife
    is done;
Rest for every faithful servant when the battle shall be won.

Tell her of that glorious waking on Thine own bright Easter day,
When the curse of sin and sorrow from our earth shall pass away;
And Thy Light—the Light Eternal—shines upon the soul for aye!

Clare

Draw back the curtain, friend, and let me see
    Mine own grey Minster,—while the mellow gleam
Gilds here and there the time-worn tracery;
    Mark, in each crumbling cleft and rugged seam
The amber lichens gather,—and the moss
    Hath spread its velvet tufts of greenest shade,
While the strong ivy-fibres reach across
    The fretted stone-work of the grim façade.

Beneath its peaceful shadow have I dwelt,
    And loved it, Gilbert, with no common love;
Often within its hallowed walls I knelt,
    Until some God-sent message, as a dove,
Flew down, and laid upon my troubled breast
    A tender promise like an olive-leaf;
And I grew quiet with the sense of rest,
    Learning to bear my lightened load of grief.

It was a morning in young June, the clouds
    Flecked the blue sky like snowflakes touched with gold
And garrulous rooks, in sable-pinioned crowds,
    Compassed the swaying elm-boughs, green and old;
Perched on the broken dial, the peacock spread
    His burnished plumage in the sun-lit air,—
When o'er the shaven lawn my sister led
    My gentle ward—the lonely orphan Clare.

She was the daughter of mine oldest friend,
    And I had vowed this sacred trust to take;
To watch the girl, and evermore defend
    Her early womanhood, for Edgar's sake;
And oft I wondered, ere I saw her face,
    How she would bear the long unbroken hours
Of dreamy quiet in this ancient place,
    Beneath the shadow of the Minster towers.

Clare

I saw the warm light touch each sombre fold
    Of her black garments as they swept the green,
I caught the glitter on the wavy gold
    Of her bright hair, and marvelled at her mien
So grave, and yet so child-like; then she raised
    Her earnest hazel eyes, dark-lashed, and deep
With sweet, unspoken thoughts; and as I gazed,
    My soul leaped up, and broke its tranquil sleep!

The weeks went on, and as they passed, she grew
    More beautiful amid the hush and gloom;
To these old dusky rooms she brought the dew
    And simple freshness of her girlish bloom;
And like some flower by summer breezes sown
    In the grey crevice of a mouldering wall,
She blossomed in my heart, unguessed, unknowns,
    And flourished there, my love, my life, my all.

I was a scholar, Gilbert; through long nights
    My study lamp burned brightly, while I found
Eternal truths, and infinite delights
    In strange black-lettered volumes, quaintly bound:
But now the teachings of a bygone age
    Lost the old charm that used to linger there,
I ceased to read—for Love had blurred the page,
    And only left thereon the name of Clare.

One golden day I sat amid my books,
    With mullioned windows opened to the morn;
And heard the ceaseless clamour of the rooks,
    And saw the yellow waves of ripened corn,
And drank the sweetness of the balmy air,
    And watched the clear light filtered through green bowers
When suddenly the silver tones of Clare
    Came drifting to me with the scent of flowers.

"I am so young, dear Raymond, and my life
    Is calm and peaceful in its level flow,

I am so young—the duties of a wife
   Are far too heavy for my years, I know;
Be patient, Raymond." Then a passionate tone
   Came trembling through the mazy screen of leaves;
"I cannot wait, my darling—be mine own,
   I cannot rest—my spirit chafes and grieves!"

Across my heart there crept a deadly chill,
   A slow sick faintness, numbing nerve and brain;
I shivered in the sunshine, and sat still,
   And knew that cries and prayers must all be vain:
Familiar sights and sounds were changed to me,
   The crows' loud voices took a mocking tone;
The golden grain stood blighted on the lea,
   The odorous south-wind whispered like a moan.

     •   •   •   •   •

Ere the white snow-shroud wrapped our woods and dells,
   I was a wanderer in other lands;
I waited not to hear the wedding-bells,
   I could not look upon their claspèd hands;
I would not mar their bliss—no sigh of mine
   Should cloud Love's mirror with the breath of care;
Alone I drained my draught of deadly wine,
   And left the sweet for Raymond and for Clare.

     •   •   •   •   •

I lingered long in Rome, eternal Rome,
   Rich in old glory, fair with ancient grace!
I stood, all hushed, beneath Saint Peter's dome,
   And gazed straight up into that dreamy space,
Hazy with golden light, and angel-wings;
   And beautiful with countless rainbow gems,
As if an untold multitude of kings
   Had lavished here their regal diadems.

Clare

I knelt on that illimitable plain
    Of many-coloured marbles, and afar
Heard the low murmur of a chanted strain,
    Or caught the glimmer of a taper-star
Before some distant shrine,—and soft clouds curled
    And hovered dimly in that luminous height;
While slowly the Cathedral of the World
    Dawned in its vastness on my dazzled sight.

I saw old marble gods grown dim with time,
    Shine still in their imperishable youth;
Born of immortal genius, and sublime
    With the great majesty and charm of truth:
I saw sweet faces smile from palace walls,
    Bright with the deathless bloom, and tender gleam
That through long ages ever softly falls
    On the rare beauty of an artist dream.

And then I left the city, when the breath
    Of summer crept amid suburban shades;
I fled the flowery paradise where Death
    Haunts the sweet twilight of the green arcades,
And sought pure air on lofty hills, vine-clad,
    Hearing the vesper bells on dewy eves
Ring their soft chimes, half mystical, half sad,
    From convent belfries framed in bowers of leaves.

    •   •   •   •   •

I could not rest, ay me,—I could not rest,
    Strange, fitful yearnings filled this soul of mine!
Heavings of troublous heart-waves, unrepress't,
    Drove me a pilgrim unto Palestine:
I saw the palmy valley of old Nile,
    And from the vast grey Pyramid looked down
On tawny sand outstretching mile on mile,
    On desert slopes, and lowlands flat and brown.

But I forgot awhile my secret pain,
    Forgot the grief that made me desolate;
When with full heart, bare brow, and slackened rein,
    I rode all slowly through Saint Stephen's Gate,
For I was in Jerusalem;—the thought
    Brought sudden thrills, and tears fell unawares,
Touched with strange light from holy memories caught;
    My soul was pregnant with unuttered prayers.

Mutely beneath the azure sky's clear heat,
    I trod in reverent love the Dolorous Way;
I see it now;—the narrow, dreary street,
    Hemmed in with ruins, spanned by arches grey!
Here toiled those blessèd Feet so wearily,—
    Here failed the feeble step and tortured limb;—
'Twas here He bore that cruel Cross for me,
    And should I shrink to bear my cross for Him?

Ah friend, my heart is faint, my voice grows weak!
    I have no words for that divinest awe
Which overshadowed me,—I cannot speak
    Of those old scenes, and all I felt and saw,
For human language fails; yet this I know,
    That my small sorrows and poor trivial strife
Sank to the very dust,—abased,—laid low,
    By the great Vision of that Perfect Life!

    •   •   •   •   •

Then I came back to England. Dim, sweet hopes
    Sprang in my silent breast like white spring flowers;
When first I saw again the fresh brown slopes,
    The windy tree-tops, and the Minster towers:
But still I trembled, for strange news bad crost
    The seas to reach me;—of a heart deceived,
A false vow broken, and a light love lost;—
    And Clare ——, I knew not if she pined or grieved.

Clare

She gave me welcome at the very door,
    Framed in the soft grey gloom she, smiling, stood,
With a rare radiance,—paler than of yore,
    And statelier with the grace of womanhood:
The bright head with its crown of shining gold;
    The dark eyes, luminous, and clear as dew;
The brow, quiescent as in days of old;
    The mobile lips, so stainless and so true.

Time cannot change the picture, nor impart
    One dusky shadow to that angel face;
Fast locked within the casket of my heart,
    Its fresh, pure colours show no fading trace:
O wedded life, so beautiful and brief,
    O calm, sweet days of summer blossoming;
O love, thrice fairer in its falling leaf,
    Than in the budding promise of its spring!

Buried beneath those ancient Minster towers,
    And I, the old man, left to die alone!
And yet not lonely; through these languid hours
    Drifts the low music of a spirit-tone;
I wait till God reveals her to my sight,
    While airy hands clasp mine, and kisses fall
On my worn brow like rays of tender light,
    That touch and tint some pallid marble wall.

'Tis twilight now, all hushed and cool and grey,
    The dusk grows deeper in this quiet room;
All care has faded with the dying day,
    Gone is the pain, the weakness, and the gloom
Friend, spread the pillow for my weary head,
    I know that I shall sleep in peace tonight;
How dark it is! Who was it sung or said
    Those words, "At evening time it shall be light"?

The Island Grave

"Right dear in the sight of the Lord is the death of His saints."

Far, far away, there lies a lonely isle,
    Whose barren shores enfold a quiet grave;
The soil is sterile there, no blossoms smile
    Upon the mound, and no green branches wave,

With gentle stirring of a leafy shade,
    To cast a shifting pattern on the turf,—
No droning insect-music there is made;
    No murmur save the ocean's moaning surf.

Only the sad sea-voice which evermore,
    Like a full heart, essays to tell its pain,
And spends its wail upon the rocky shore
    That flings the mournful story back again.

No loving faces bend that tomb above,
    No fond hands touch the stone with tender care;
And yet God only knows the mighty love,
    And all the bright hopes that are buried there.

He only knows how truly, day by day,
    One widowed heart that memory must keep,
Teaching the sweet child-voices, when they pray,
    To speak their father's name before they sleep.

He only knows the earnest, yearning gaze
    Of patient eyes, whose tears in silence fall,
When the first morning sunbeam sends its rays
    To gild one pictured face upon the wall.

Yet from Despair's dry soil how Faith springs up,
    As a pure fountain leaps to meet the sun!
The lips that once said, "Take away this cup,"
    Are the same lips that say, "Thy will be done."

Thy will be done, O Lord! A little while,
    A few more years of patience and of prayer,

The Island Grave

And then the grave upon that lonely isle
    Shall give her back the treasure hidden there.

For Thou didst take away death's keenest sting,
    Lord Jesus, when Thy precious blood was shed;
The crimson Cross, the shame, the suffering,
    Have won the Resurrection of the dead.

Alas for us, if with that fluttering breath
    From lips belovèd, all indeed were o'er,
If Hope itself laid down and died with Death,
    And human love dared look for nothing more.

But Christ, by that great sacrifice of thine,
    The lost shall be restored to longing eyes;
With a "new body" glorified, divine,
    The dead who "sleep in Jesus" shall arise.

The voice of Thine Archangel shall arouse
    The saints who calmly rest in earth or sea,
When Thou shalt come, O Bridegroom, to Thy Spouse,
    And take Thy ransomed loved ones home with Thee.

Twilight in a Minster

I lingered in a dim Cathedral nave,
    And watched the dusk across the marble floor
Creep silently, as glides the stealthy wave
    Over the gleaming pebbles of the shore.

The shadows of that winter eventide
    Shrouded the glory of the solemn choir,
Save where the chancel windows, ruby-dyed,
    Burned like the embers of a fading fire.

No sudden strain of organ-notes awoke
    Within my soul the melody of prayer,
No silver burst of chanting voices broke
    The utter stillness that was reigning there.

But as I stood within that ancient fane
    A wondrous peace upon my spirit fell,
A sense of rest to soothe the weary brain,
    A bliss that I can find no words to tell.

I thought of those whose earnest toil and strength
    Had shaped each sacred stone and found its place,
Till the whole building fitly framed at length
    Was perfect in its majesty and grace.

I thought of all the blessed ones who trod
    The time-worn pavement with such patient feet;
Now are they numbered with the saints of God,
    Now in the rest of paradise they meet.

Ay, where I stood they oft had knelt to pray,
    On those grey stones their tears of sorrow fell,
When men had wandered from the one true way,
    And storms assailed the church they loved so well.

Here was the benediction often poured
    On yearning hearts like dew on thirsty sod;

Here did they take the Body of their Lord,
    And drank the everlasting wine of God.

And as I mused, I seemed to see the shades
    Of those old worshippers of days gone by;
They gathered softly in the long arcades
    Like evening clouds that haunt the western sky.

Bishops and priests and virgins slowly swept
    In vast procession through those arches dim;
I saw their tranquil faces, and I wept
    For very joy to hear their holy hymn.

"O praise the Lord," they chanted as they passed,
    "Praise Him, ye angels, praise Him, stars and light";
Thus sung they like a silver trumpet-blast,
    "Praise Him, ye heavens, praise Him in the height!"

Oft in her loneliness my soul recalls
    That vision in the Minster far away;
The strain that fancy heard within those walls
    Shall echo through my memory for aye,—

To give me calmness in the world's turmoil,
    And courage if the battle should be sore;
Until I reach the end of earthly toil,
    And in life's twilight hear that song once more.

Thanksgiving Hymn

While the earth remaineth, seedtime and harvest, and cold and heat, and summer and winter, and day and night shall not cease.
— GENESIS 8:22.

Praised be the Lord most holy,
    Throned above His mercy-seat!
He hath blest us, great and lowly,
    Filled us with the flour of wheat;
Making peace within our borders,
    Making life and labour sweet.

He hath blest us on the mountains,
    He hath blest us in the vales,
Watered us in silver fountains,
    Breathed on us in balmy gales;
Lo! the earth brings forth her treasures,
    For His promise never fails!

Farther still His love extendeth,
    Higher yet His bounties rise;
With the Living Bread He sendeth,
    Hungry souls he satisfies:
And the children of the kingdom
    Draw from Him their rich supplies.

Watch us! O almighty Maker!
    Watch the seed that Thou hast sown;
Grant that many a fruitful acre
    Thine abundant care may own:
Hasten, Lord, that day of reaping,
    When Thine increase shall be shown.

Though the tempest of temptation
    Beats across Thy field below—
Guard the fruits of Thy salvation!
    Wheat and tares together grow,

But the Master of the harvest
   All His blessed grain shall know.

Father, when Thine angel, reapers
   Come to reap Thy precious store—
When Thy call awakes the sleepers
   Given back from sea and shore—
Safe within the golden garner
   Gather us for evermore!
               Amen.

Rest

Wide fields and moors in russet garments vested;
 A lone hill lifted calm and still and fair
Above the darkening haze, and faintly crested
 With tender brightness in the moonlit air.

Brown, withered leaves, some shelter mutely craving,
 Lie heaped in clefts and hollows of the bank
Whose scarlet berries gleam, and fern plumes waving
 Shadow the mossy velvet, green and dank.

Over the trees a silver network, airy
 And delicate as woven ray of light,
Wrought by the fingers of some silent fairy,
 In the clear moonshine of an autumn night.

I listen,—for this quiet wind is singing
 A penitential psalm in undertones,
Breathing faint sadness in its sighs, and swinging
 The solemn fir-tree, crowned with clustered cones.

I know not why the stillness and the sweetness
 Of nights like this bring out that subtle sense
Of our own life's mysterious incompleteness,
 Its little knowledge, and its sad pretence.

O that the calm of God were resting lightly
 On weary spirit and on striving hand,
Like these soft beams of light that shed so brightly
 A Sabbath quiet over all the land!

O, to be hushed and feel His presence shining
 Around our lives, to keep them pure and still,
To stay our feverèd and eager pining,
 And trust in meekness to His holy will!

Earth hath her times of peace,—we struggle vainly,
 In ceaseless action, toiling to be blest;
This autumn calm may show us all too plainly,
 Our restlessness that chafes against God's rest.

After the Storm

Patience! for the strife is o'er;
 Weary wave and dying blast
Beat and moan around the shore;
 Peace must come at last.

Lo! the seagull's silver wing
 Flashes in the sunset gold;
Wait, another morn shall bring
 Gladness, as of old.

Sunlight on the yellow strand,
 Shadows lying still and clear;
Pearly fringes on the sand;
 Murmurs, sweet to hear.

Storms of life must have their way
 Ere these changeful years may cease;
Foam and tempest for today,
 And tomorrow—peace.

Children of the Mountain

Child of the mountain, thy home on the heights
    Lures thee afar from our summer-crowned vale;
Here thou art weary of languid delights,
    Longing in vain for the song of the gale;

Faint with the sweetness of myrtles and vines,
    Tired of the burden and heat of the day,
Still in thy musing the voice of the pines
    Sighs to thy spirit, and calls thee away!

Only one friend from that wild mountain spot
    Clings to thee yet in thy loneliest hours,
Only the ewe that was born near thy cot
    Follows thy footsteps through leaf-shaped bowers.

O'er the lone passes that glitter with snow
    Once she came gaily to bound by thy side,
Now in the walks where the red roses glow,
    Still she is faithful whatever betide.

Gentle and steadfast she bears with her fate,
    Here in the valley contented to be;
Learn by her patience to quietly wait
    For the bright days that are coming to thee.

Good Night

Good night, good night, the day is slowly dying,
  Home flits the swallow to the cottage eaves;
A little wind creeps through the woodland, sighing,
  And dies among the leaves.

The red deer seeks the bracken in the dingle,
  The flocks are couching on their beds of thyme;
Far off, a long wave rolls upon the shingle,
  And sings its sleepy rhyme.

Oh, rest in peace; our angel-guards, unsleeping,
  Watch o'er the homes where languid sorrow lies;
After the darkness of a night of weeping,
  The morn of joy shall rise!

Good night, good night; in quiet chambers kneeling,
  We pray for our beloved ones out of sight;
There comes an answer through the cool air stealing,
  "God bless you, love, good night."

Thanksgiving for the New Year

I bless Thee, gracious Father, meekly kneeling
    Before Thee, while the Old Year softly dies,
In this calm hour mine inmost soul revealing
    To Thy most holy eyes.

I bless Thee for the sad year's labor ended,
    And for the strength that made my burdens light;
I praise Thee for the tender hands extended
    Over my home tonight.

I bless Thee for the love that chastened kindly
    My wilful spirit in the days of old,
When I, Thy wayward child, was choosing blindly
    The dross before the gold!

I bless Thee for the voice of consolation,
    That speaks, in gentlest tones, of pardoned sin,
And bids me strive, through sorrow and temptation,
    My golden cross to win.

Oh, for His sake whose love all love excelleth,
    Extend Thy care through coming nights and days;
And from the place wherein Thine honor dwelleth,
    Receive this New Year's praise!

"At the Last"

In the silence, and the twilight,
  Sad I sit, and lone;
Brooding o'er the griefs, the losses,
  That my life has known.
Loss of wealth, of friends, of pleasures,
  (These things were but small):
But my soul had dearer treasures,
  And I lost them all.

Once I had a wife—how cherished,
  Loving to the last;
Just when most I seemed to need her,
  From my world she passed!
I was left to toil—forsaken—
  While her rest was won;
Yet, I said, with faith unshaken:
  "Lord, Thy will be done!"

At the last, thank God! I'll find them—
  Friend, and wife, and trust;
When the mortal veil about me
  Changes into dust.
Through the quiet twilight creeping,
  Comes an angel's tone:
"They are in a better keeping,
  Thou shalt claim thine own."

Baby's Grave

In the church-yard, in the shadow,
 Baby sleeps;
While the wind, from wood and meadow,
 Softly weeps.
O'er the little mound we made him—
 God knows best,
With what aching hearts we laid him
 Down to rest.

Vain the tears and prayers we offered—
 He has slept,
While we lived, and toiled, and suffered,
 Grieved and wept.
God was wisest. Who can number
 All the woe,
Baby, in his tranquil slumber,
 Does not know.

Bringing Home the Flock

Through pastures fair,
And sea-girt paths all wild with rock and foam,
O'er velvet sward, and desert stern and bare,
    The flock comes home.

A weary way,
Now smooth, then rugged with a thousand snares,
Now dim with rain, then sweet with blossoms gay
    And summer's airs.

Yet, safe at last,
Within the fold they gather, and are still;
Sheltered from driving shower and stormy blast,
    They fear no ill.

Through life's dark ways,
Through flowery paths where evil angels roam,
Through restless nights, and long, heart-wasting days,
    Christ's flock comes home.

Safe to the fold,
The happy fold, where fears are never known,
Love-guarded, fenced about with walls of gold,
    He leads His own.

O shepherd-king,
With wounded hands, whose slightest touch is blest!
Thine is the kingdom, Thine the power, to bring
    Thy flock to rest!

In the People's Garden

Oh, the linden boughs are swinging
　　As the wind sighs from the west;
I can hear the children singing,
　　But the zephyr's song is best;
Little hearts laugh out their gladness,
　　Long may their life-music last;
Ah, what can they know of sadness,
　　For the children have no past!
But the west wind murmurs faintly
　　To the blossoms of the lime,
"It was in the people's garden,
　　And the year was in its prime."

It was in the people's garden
　　That your love to me was told,
Ere your heart began to harden,
　　And your face grew false and cold;
We were workers, bred together
　　In a sordid city street,
Humble birds of common feather,
　　Life was hard, but love was sweet;
We were patient, asking only
　　Longer rest and better pay;
And the end was clear before us,
　　When you chose another way.

You were handsome, you were clever,
　　You could win the rich man's ear;
You were eloquent, yet never
　　Told your brethren's hope and fear;
Now your wealthy masters prize you,
　　And you ride where once you ran;
I, the working-girl, despise you—
　　You, the self-made gentleman!
Poor and weary and forsaken,

In the People's Garden

Lone and blighted in my youth,
I have still the faithful spirit
  That is true to God and truth.

Hark, from many a city steeple
  Bells are calling clear and high,
And the daughter of the people
  Hears their eager souls reply;
What is this that they are crying
  Under God's great azure dome?
"Right the wrong, and save the dying,
  Come, and make the world Thy home!
Make this earth Thy people's garden,
  Free from want and woe and crime,
We are waiting, hoping, praying,
  Come, and bring our golden time!"

Pansies

I send thee pansies while the year is young,
    Yellow as sunshine, purple as the night;
Flowers of remembrance, ever fondly sung
    By all the chiefest of the Sons of Light;
And if in recollection lives regret
    For wasted days and dreams that were not true,
I tell thee that the "pansy freaked with jet"
    Is still the heart's-ease that the poets knew.
Take all the sweetness of a gift unsought,
    And for the pansies send me back a thought.

"Of the Earth, Earthy"

Have they told you I am going
 To the land of rest?
I am very patient, knowing
 All is for the best;
Yet the summer light is clearest
 Ere the soul departs,
Nature seems to draw the nearest
 Unto dying hearts.

Have they told you I am leaving
 Earthly things behind?
Love, perhaps, was but deceiving,
 Friendship proved unkind;
Yet the sunshine, softly stealing
 Down the soft green slope,
Brings back all the trustful feeling,
 All the dreams of hope.

Have they told you I am hasting
 To a fairer home?
Yes; but here are roses wasting,
 Blossoms white as foam;
Here are sun-gilt vine-leaves wreathing
 Round our cottage door;
Here the solemn fir-trees breathing
 Fragrance evermore.

Have they told you I am setting
 All my thoughts on high?
Yes; but can I learn forgetting
 While old haunts are nigh?
When the bracken plumes are swaying
 On our pine-crown'd hill,
I can almost hear you saying
 That you love me still.

Hush! I hear a footstep falling
    On the garden plot,
And a voice speaks, softly calling,
    Yet I answer not
Till I feel your arms around me,
    On my face your breath.
Love and faith have sought and found me;
    This is life—not death.

In the Cloisters

An ancient English city,—and a grave,
   Beneath the shadow of cathedral walls,
Where solemn elms their bowery branches wave,
   And tender rain of April softly falls;
Hoarse-voiced rooks,—a restless sable crowd,—
   Whirl with strange clangour round the bleak old towers,
Drifting and meeting, closing like a cloud
   Above grim bosses and grey stone-wrought flowers.

Great mouldering heights of rugged sculpture rise,
   Grisly with heads of dragons,—worn and bold,
Coloured by weather-stains of thousand dyes,
   Tinged with the lichen's melancholy gold;
While here and there some shattered saint looks down
   From his dark niche betwixt the pillars high,
Or stately king still wears his stony crown,
   And with calm brow confronts the changeful sky.

There, on that lowly grave, the snowdrop springs,
   There smile the dim blue violets of March;
And like a sound of mighty rushing wings
   Through the low western doorway's pointed arch
Sweeps forth the deep prayer-music o'er the mound,
   And dies far out amid the busy strife
Beyond the minster-gates,—where toil hath drowned
   The faint sweet echoes of eternal Life.

Soft moss of shady green and pearly grey
   Has clustered thickly on the time-worn stone;
Dark ivy-chains, that strengthen day by day,
   About the grave their clasping bonds have thrown;
And often I go back through misty years
   Along dim paths where love's old wild-flowers grow,
To seek that sheltered place with quiet tears
   Where one true heart was buried long ago.

Love and Money

"Love is potent, but money is omnipotent."

Out in the twilight, alone in the lane,
All the old sweetness steals o'er me again;
All the old longing, forgotten of late,
Stirs in my heart as I stand at her gate;
Silent and dim is the cottage tonight,
Smothered in roses, cream-tinted and white;
Jasmine blossoms besprinkle the sod,
Dusky and still are the paths that she trod.
Oh, for one moment to meet her, and see
Just the old look, that shone only for me!
Why am I sighing here—what can I do?
"L'amour fait beaucoup, mais l'argent fait tout."

Little white Rose, there were true knights of old—
Heroes who counted Love dearer than gold;
Men with strong arms, who could fight for their way;
Why were we born in this world of today?
Why does society smite with a sneer
Wretches who wed on three hundred a year?
Why—But a truce to these follies of mine!
I am no knight of the days of lang syne;
Only a lounger with duns at his heels,
Only a dreamer who maunders and feels,
Only a trifler who sighs after you;
"L'amour fait beaucoup, mais l'argent fait tout."

Safe in the cottage that nobody knows,
Sleep, and forget me, my little white Rose!
Heartsick and weary, I turn from your gate,
Tired of the strife betwixt passion and Fate;
There will be parting and pain if we meet:
Better to leave you than grieve you, my sweet;
Ay, it is true, as some poets can tell,
Love is best proved by a silent farewell.

Love and Money

Out in the starlight I wander again,
Through the deep gloom of the oak-shadowed lane,
Back to the crowd that cares nothing for you;
"L'amour fait beaucoup, mais l'argent fait tout."

Just for Tonight

Softly the Summer day fades on the sea;
Faintly the vesper-wind murmurs to me,
Murmurs and sighs of the sunsets of old
When we were turning life's "pages of gold";
Then in love's madness we turned them too fast,
Yet there is one golden leaf for the last:
Listen, the ebbing wave gathers and breaks,
How it caresses the strand it forsakes,
Sprinkling the pebbles with flashes of light!—
Leave me tomorrow, love, kiss me tonight.

We were but dreamers and idlers, they say,
In the bright hours that have drifted away;
Well, let them say so;—in sorrow and pain
All the old gladness will come back again:
Just for tonight, while the west is aglow,
Shall we not love as we loved long ago?
Only one blossom is left on the bough,
Shall we not seize on its loveliness now?
Let the last hour be a mournful delight,
Leave me tomorrow, but kiss me tonight.

Ay, we were weak when we should have been brave.
I was a trifler and you were a slave;
Chances slipped by, and we saw them too late,
Friends played us false, and we said it was fate:
Only this moment is ours ere it dies,
What if that setting sun never should rise?
What if this life with its sweetness and fear
Closes for ever, and ends for us here?
Somewhere, far off, in a new world of light
Love has its morrow; then kiss me tonight.

Cleopatra to Antony

Spread a feast with choicest viands—
    Friends, 't will be my very last;
Bring the rarest flowers to grace it—
    Haste, my sands of life flow fast;
Place an asp beneath the lotus
    That shall light me to the grave
With its starry petals' splendor;
    Weep not, let your hearts be brave.

Speed, Octavia, with thy minions—
    Fire thy heart with deadly hate!
Thou wilt miss the royal victim—
    Cleopatra rules her fate!
She defies Rome's conquering legions!
    Let them triumph in her fall!
What is earthly pomp or greatness?—
    Love, thy love outweighs it all!

Thrones and sceptres are but trifles
    To my spirit's yearning pain;
What were fortune's gifts without *thee*
    I would lose the world to gain?
Let no base heart tell our story;
    Ages, speak, when time unurns
These dull ashes, say to Ages,
    Soul to soul their love still burns.

Fatal asp, thy sleep's not endless,
    That the morrow's dawn will prove;
I shall reign in lands elysian,
    Antony's proud Queen of Love!
Isis and Osiris, hear me!
    Hear me, gods of boundless power!
Ye have tasted deathless passion!
    Ye will guide me to his bower!

Cleopatra to Antony

Pardon, mighty ones, the error
    If Octavia I have wronged,
Judged by higher laws supernal;
    Ah! how earthly passions thronged.
Overpowering heart and reason,
    Nature, answering Nature's call,
Rushed as cloud responsive rushes
    On to cloud, to meet and—fall.

Antony, my love, I'm dying!
    Curdles fast life's crimson tide,
But no dark Plutonian shadows
    Fall between us to divide.
Hark! the Stygian waters swelling,
    Call me, love, with thee to rest,—
Death I fear not since thou braved it,
    Pillowed on my aching breast.

Strange emotions fill my bosom
    As I near the vast unknown;
Yet my heart still throbs in dying,
    Antony, for thee alone.
Oh! "I feel immortal longings,"—
    I can brave stern Pluto's frown,—
Robe me in my regal garments,
    Deck with jewels, sceptre, crown.

Antony! I'm coming! coming!
    Open, open wide thine arms!
Ah! the blissful hope or union
    Robs the grave of its alarms.
See! the glorious heroes beckon
    O'er the Stygian water's swell.
I shall have immortal crowning!
    Egypt—dear old Nile!—farewell.

What Life Hath

Life hath its barren years,
When blossoms fall untimely down,
When ripened fruitage fails to crown
The summer toil, when Nature's frown
   Looks only on our tears.

Life hath its faithless days—
The golden promise of the morn,
That seemed for light and gladness born,
Mean only noontide wreck and scorn,
   Hushed harp instead of praise.

Life hath its valleys too,
Where we must walk with vain regret,
With mourning clothed, with wild rain wet—
Towards sunlit hopes that soon must set,
   All quenched in pitying dew.

Life hath its harvest moons,
Its tasselled corn and purple-weighted vine,
Its gathered sheaves of grain, the blessed sign
Of plenteous ripening, bread, and pure, rich wine;
   Full hearts for harvest tunes.

Life hath its hopes fulfilled,
Its glad fruitions, its blessed answered prayers,
Sweeter for waiting long whose holy air,
Indrawn to silent souls, breathes forth its rare,
   Grand speech by joy distilled.

Life hath its Tabor heights,
Its lofty mounts of heavenly recognition,
Whose unveiled glories flash to earth, munition
Of love and truth and clear intuition.
   Hail! mount of all delights.

Some Words

Only some words about the dear old times,
　　Spoken amid the clamor of the street,
But they were like the music of the chimes
　　Drifting across the meadows, faintly sweet.

Only some words from one who knew the past,
　　Whose eyes had seen the light of suns gone down.
Such simple words! and yet a spell was cast
　　Upon the tumult of the noisy town.

I saw once more the home among the hills,
　　The lights and shadows on the quiet way,
The budding boughs, the gold of daffodils,
　　The long, soft grasses waving all the day.

The shades grew deeper, and, behold, I dreamed
　　A dream of summer woods in gloom and glow.
Leaves changed and fell, and scarlet berries gleamed,
　　Dropping, like coral beads, on heaps of snow.

Only some words; but neither brush nor pen
　　Could paint such pictures for any weary eyes.
Beyond the crowd—beyond the strife of men—
　　I looked, and saw those lovely visions rise.

Such simple words! But words are mighty things;
　　They cast us down, or lift us up to rest:
They charm and strengthen, till our angel sings
　　The last of all the life-songs, and the best.

Great Tom of Oxford

A Song of the Bell

The day is ended, the night steals down
    On alley and hall and street,
And over the roofs of the storied town
    The bell tolls, solemn and sweet;
They close the doors at that grave old voice,
    And they make the portals fast;
For the sad may sigh, and the gay rejoice,
    But the night must fall at last.

Oh, tuneful Tom, in your belfry lone,
    Above our clamour and strife,
The prayer that thrills in your golden tone
    Comes back from a vanished life;
From faithful hearts that have passed away
    (Great hearts, so tender and deep!)
You speak to the feverish souls today,
    Who strive and waver and weep.

What have you learnt in the silence, Bell,
    Shut in by your window-bars?
Have you heard far off, where saints may dwell,
    The song of the morning stars?
Do you mark the angel's downward sweep,
    And the spirit's upward flight?
Do you know who wakes while the children sleep?
    Ho, watchman, what of the night!

Sing us the song of the shining ones,
    The song of the age of gold;
Beyond the roar of the distant guns
    Its glorious strains have rolled;
And some are dreaming a dream of peace
    Down here in the world of sin;
Is there never a hope that war may cease,
    And a holier life begin?

Great Tom of Oxford

Above the roofs of the storied town,
    And over the river's flow,
While youth and vigour, in cap and gown,
    Are thronging the streets below,
Toll on, Great Tom, in your lonely tower,
    O'er meadow and ford and fen;
Strike deeper and deeper, with solemn power,
    To quicken the souls of men.

Snowdrops—Consolation

A small bird twitters on a leafless spray,
    Across the snow-waste breaks a gleam of gold:
What token can I give my friend today
    But February blossoms, pure and cold?
Frail gifts from Nature's half-reluctant hand,
    What if he deems them meaningless and pale?
I see the signs of spring about the land,
    I hear in dreams the cuckoo's summer tale;
And these chill snowdrops, fresh from wintry bowers,
    Are the forerunners of a world of flowers.

The Last Snow of Winter

Soft snow still rests within this wayside cleft,
    Veiling the primrose buds not yet unfurled;
Last trace of dreary winter, idly left
    On beds of moss, and sere leaves crisply curled;
Why does it linger while the violets blow,
                    And sweet things grow?

A relic of long nights and weary days,
    When all fair things were hidden from my sight;
A chill reminder of those mournful ways
    I traversed when the fields were cold and white;
My life was dim, my hopes lay still and low
                    Beneath the snow.

Now spring is coming, and my buried love
    Breaks fresh and strong and living through the sod;
The lark sings loudly in the blue above,
    The budding earth must magnify her God;
Let the old sorrows and old errors go
                    With the last snow.

My Confidence

I hold Thy truth, O Lord, within my heart,
    Thy law I love;
I hold Thy cross, and try to do my part
    My faith to prove;
I hold Thy promise, Lord, and daily pray
    "My faith increase,
That I may closer cleave to Thee, the Way,
    And have Thy peace."
Yet little joy my holding brings to me,
    Because I know
That, though my soul still trusting clings to Thee,
    I may let go.

But I am held, O Lord; Thou hast my hand,
    And Thou art strong;
Throughout my journey in this desert land,
    However long,
Thou givest me support. I shall not fall.
    Though foes assail
And press me hard, over myself and all,
    I shall prevail.
Great joy Thy presence and Thy pledge afford,
    Because I know
That Thou wilt not, since Thou hast given Thy word,
    Of me let go.

When the Boats Come Home

There's light upon the sea today,
  And gladness on the strand;
Ah! well ye know that hearts are gay
  When sails draw nigh the land!
We followed them with thoughts and tears,
  Far, far across the foam;
Dear Lord, it seems a thousand years
  Until the boats come home!

We tend the children, live our life,
  And toil, and mend the nets;
But is there ever maid or wife
  Whose faithful heart forgets?
We know what cruel dangers lie
  Beneath that shining foam,
And watch the changes in the sky
  Until the boats come home.

There's glory on the sea today,
  The sunset gold is bright;
Methought I heard a grandsire say,
  "At eve it shall be light!"
O'er waves of crystal touched with fire,
  And flakes of pearly foam,
We gaze and see our hearts' desire—
  The boats are coming home.

Entered into Rest

March 3ʳᵈ, 1871

"And I look for the resurrection of the dead:
and the life of the world to come."

As one who pauses in the fevered heat
    Of city toil, to muse with yearning brain
On some calm Sunday, spent in cool retreat
    Of sylvan shades he may not view again.

Living those golden hours of praise anew,
    And dreaming of the peace that follows prayer,
When solemnly the red light died in dew,
    And tender perfumes wandered through the air.

So pausing in our busy lives, we turn
    To those fair days when thou wert with us yet,
Whose lingering glories in our spirits burn
    So brightly that we scarce can know regret.

We live again the quiet, calm delight
    Of sweet communion held on summer eves,
When thought met thought, like odours drawn by night
    From sighing blossoms and from rustling leaves.

But often, in that happy, vanished time,
    Came pauses in the music of thy speech,
As if thine ears had caught some holy chime,
    That ever failed our duller sense to reach.

Death had been near thee in the far-off land
    Where foes were vanquished on their native soil;
Thine was the stalwart front, the ready hand,
    And thine the guerdon of the soldier's toil.

The pestilence that walketh in the night,
    The winged shaft that flieth in the day,
Were near thee, but an unseen arm of might
    Warded the deadly perils from thy way.

Spared in the strife upon the battle plain,
   Saved in the stormy dangers of the wave;
Guarded from hungry sword and restless main,
   To find at last a quiet English grave.

A tranquil resting-place, where soft winds bear
   The scent of heather from the breezy down;
And hands that soothed thee with love's earnest care,
   Now deck thy mound with floral cross and crown.

While from the old church portal faintly strays
   Some ancient melody once held so dear,
A chant of prayer, or triumph song of praise,
   That cheered thee in thine hours of sorrow here.

Under the shadow of our mother's wing,
   Sleeping in peace until that morn shall break,
When Christ, the Living Conqueror and King,
   Comes in His godly might, and bid to thee wake.

Thine was the blessed hope, the simple trust,
   That saw His glory when thy light grew dim,
That felt His mercy lift thee from the dust,
   And clasp thee in thy weakness close to Him.

Thine was the courage that His strength bestowed,
   The patience born of sorrow sanctified;
No fears assailed thee on the quiet road
   That led thy footsteps to the riverside.

The solemn river,—that the saints have crossed
   At dawn and eventide, at noon and night;
Some with untroubled souls, some tempest-tossed,
   But all with that bright land before their sight.

We fain would follow,—and the prayer-words flow,
   Broken and faint, and tremulous with tears;
"How long, O Lord, shall last these days of woe,
   This weary record of slow-gliding years?"

Soft comes the answer, sweet as summer's breath;
  "If ye believe in God believe in Me;
Lo! I have overcome the sting of death,
  And where I am, there shall My servants be."

NOTE.—In memory of a young English officer, who having seen active Service, and greatly distinguished himself abroad; returned to his home to die of decline in his twenty-ninth year.

A Lost Hour

A golden hour on a Summer morn,
  When half the world was still,
The dew was fresh on the new-mown hay,
And the bridal veil of the fair young day
  Hung o'er the purple hill.

The sheep-bells tinkled across the slopes,
  Sweet as an elfin chime;
Butterflies flitted athwart the down,
Bees went murmuring, busy and brown,
  Over the fragrant thyme.

A languid calm and a dull content,
  Silence instead of speech;
The wind sighed low, and the lark sang high,
But the golden hour of our lives went by,
  And drifted out of reach.

We both went back to an eager life;
  But in its pause today
The dream of that golden hour returns,
And my jaded spirit frets and yearns
  For one chance swept away.

The years creep on, and the heart grows tired
  Even of hopes fulfilled,
And turns away from the world's strong wine
With fevered lips that must ever pine
  For that pure draught we spilled.

And yet perchance when our long day wanes
  (Age hath its joys late-born;)
We shall meet again on the green hillside,
And find, in the solemn eventide,
  The hour we lost at morn.

A Return

The charm of the golden trees.
    The glow of the autumn day,
And the garden walks with their murm'ring bees,
    Soothe all my cares away.

My soul is sick of the strife
    Where pulses never are stilled;
But here, in the rest, of a simple life,
    God's promise is fulfilled.

When the bramble bears its fruit,
    And mists creep over the lea,
And soft as the sound of a distant flute
    The sheep-bells chime to me;

When the bracken turns to gold,
    And down in the winding lane
A little bird sings me the songs of old
    Till youth comes back again;

Then trouble and pain depart,
    And comfort and peace draw near,
And all the foes of a timorous heart
    Like phantoms disappear.

And the autumn lands grow fair
    With a light that seems divine;
And the treasures I left in childhood there,
    Once more are wholly mine.

Parting Blessing

Who hath also sealed us, and given the earnest of the Spirit in our hearts.—2 CORINTHIANS 1:22.

Saviour, now the day is ending,
And the shades of evening fall,
Let thy Holy Dove, descending,
Bring thy mercy to us all;
Set thy seal on every heart,
Jesus, bless us ere we part!

Bless the gospel message spoken,
In thine own appointed way;
Give each fainting soul a token
Of thy tender love today:
Set thy seal on every heart,
Jesus, bless us ere we part!

Comfort those in pain or sorrow
Watch each sleeping child of thine;
Let us all arise tomorrow
Strengthened by thy grace divine;
Set thy seal on every heart,
Jesus, bless us ere we part!

Pardon thou each deed unholy;
Lord, forgive each sinful thought;
Make us contrite, pure, and lowly,
By thy great example taught:
Set thy seal on every heart,
Jesus, bless us ere we part!

First Line Index

www.ingramcontent.com/pod-product-compliance
Lightning Source LLC
Chambersburg PA
CBHW060332100426
42812CB00003B/959